John & Carole Thompson

Rich in the Things That Count the Most

James W. Moore

Rich in the Things That Count the Most

DIMENSIONS
FOR LIVING
NASHVILLE

RICH IN THE THINGS THAT COUNT THE MOST

This book is printed on acid-free paper.

Library of Congress Cataloging-in-Publication Data

Moore, James W. (James Wendell), 1938-
   Rich in the things that count the most / James W. Moore.
     p. cm.
   ISBN 0-687-49010-3 (pbk. : alk. paper)
   1. Christian life—Methodist authors. I. Title.
   BV4501.3.M6643 2006
   248.4—dc22

                                                      2006015138

06 07 08 09 10 11 12 13 14 15—10 9 8 7 6 5 4 3 2 1

MANUFACTURED IN THE UNITED STATES OF AMERICA

For June, Jodi, Danny, Sarah, Paul, Jeff, Claire, Dawson, Daniel, Lily, and Kirby . . . who know what it means to be rich in the things that count the most.

Contents

Introduction

Rich in the Things That Count the Most

Scripture: Luke 19:1-10

IN ALMOST EVERY HEALTHY FAMILY, THE CHILDREN, AS THEY GROW older, like to tease their parents (especially their dads) about some funny moment from the past. The moment our children most like to tease me about happened when our daughter, Jodi, was sixteen years old. Her younger brother, Jeff, was thirteen at the time. They, grinning mischievously, came into the den of our home one evening to tell me that one of their friends named Jennifer had just turned sixteen and her dad had given her a brand new red sports car for her birthday. They both thought that this was a great idea, a great gesture on Jennifer's dad's part. They thought that Jodi, who had just turned sixteen a few days before, would be glad to receive a brand new red sports car from her dad anytime now and that Jeff would like one also when he reached sixteen years of age.

I said, "Well, let me explain that. Jennifer's father is a very successful oil man, one of the wealthiest men in town. He could easily afford a brand new sports car for his daughter, and I know that we are all happy for them and their good fortune. However, I am a Methodist minister with a Methodist minister's salary. The church has been wonderful to us, but the truth is we can't afford a brand new car right now."

Jeff, empathizing with his big sister, spoke for both of them, expressing their disappointment. He said, "Rats!" (That's about as strong as it gets in a parsonage.) He said, "Rats! I wish we were rich!" And I said, "We are rich. We are rich in the things that count the most! We have love, we have faith, we have the church, and we have one another. Those are the things in life that really matter. We can't afford a sports car right now, but we are rich in the things that count the most."

Now, Jodi and Jeff knew that and really understood that deep down inside. They knew coming in that night that the chances of a new car were slim to none. But over the years and up to the present moment, they have had such fun teasing me about that conversation. They think it's hilarious!

🖘 "We'd like to take a family cruise to Hawaii, Dad, but we can't afford it. That's OK because we are rich in the things that count-the most!"

🖘 "The World Series? The Super Bowl? The Final Four? Wimbledon? The Masters? Cabin in Colorado? No way! But that's OK because we are rich in the things that count the most."

🖘 "Dad's got a hole in his shoe, but don't worry about it, because we are rich in the things that count the most."

After each comment like that, they laugh and laugh and hug me. They think it's so funny, and yet that is precisely what they are now saying to their children when their children want something they don't really need or they can't really afford. The point is: it's nice to have money and the things that money can buy, but every now and then we need to check to be sure that we have the things money can't buy. Now, please don't misunderstand me. I am not being critical of wealthy people. As a matter of fact, I know quite a number of people, some of them my best friends, who have both. They have material wealth, and they also have the riches that count the most.

Over the years, I have noticed that the people who are rich and happy are the people who would be happy even if they weren't rich because their happiness is not dependent on material things.

I hope we will all count our many blessings and name them one by one; but as we do that, it's good to remember that even if we didn't have a lot of possessions, we could still be grateful because God is with us and God is for us. Real gratitude is more than counting material blessings. God is our friend, and that is the real source of our gratitude. That's the real reason we can be grateful.

Isn't it fascinating and revealing to note that our greatest expressions of thanksgiving historically have come from people who did not have a lot of material "things." Think about it:

🕭 Jesus, who had no place to lay his head;

🕭 Luther, who was in hiding for his life;

🕭 Francis of Assisi, who was voluntarily poor;

🕭 Helen Keller, who was blind and deaf;

🕭 Mother Teresa, who served tirelessly in a leper colony;

🕭 the Pilgrims, who were hungry, cold, and scared at Plymouth Rock.

There's a sermon there somewhere and it's all about the lesson Zacchaeus learned that day in Jericho. He was a chief tax collector and very, very rich. He was rich and miserable! Miserable because his selfish pursuit of wealth had cost him dearly. It had caused him to lose his God, his church, and his friends. His selfish pursuit of ill-gotten wealth had caused him to lose the riches of life that count the most.

Let me ask you something. What are you most grateful for today? What are the riches in your life right now that will last and endure, that won't rust or corrode or become boring or go out of style? What are the riches that Zacchaeus found that day in Jericho? What are the riches that count the most? Let me mention three that flow gracefully out of the Zacchaeus story in Luke 19.

First, There Is Faith

There is God and his amazing grace. How is it with you right now? Are you rich in faith? Are you rich in God? There's nothing more valuable than having God in your life. That's why Zacchaeus was so miserable that day in Jericho. He had lost his God. He had lost his faith. He had drifted away from his Lord, his Master, his Creator, his Savior. Even though he had great material riches that day, he felt lost and empty and unhappy.

And then look what happens. God comes looking for him. Jesus walks over to that sycamore tree, looks up, and calls him by name.

He doesn't say, "Hey, you!" or "Hey, Shorty!" or "Hey, tax collector." He calls him by name: "Zacchaeus, come on down. Let's go and have lunch together." For the rest of his life, Zacchaeus would never forget the sheer lunatic joy of that moment.

God came looking for him and came in the spirit of grace and forgiveness. God came to him and called him by name, and Zacchaeus's life was turned completely around because he suddenly realized that faith in God is the most valuable thing in the world.

Notice that Jesus gave Zacchaeus no material gifts. Jesus gave him something better—grace, respect, acceptance, forgiveness, a chance to change his life and make a new start. Zacchaeus was so touched, so honored, so grateful, that his lifestyle was totally changed. Why, it even touched his wallet: "Behold, Lord," he says, "the half of my goods I give to the poor, and if I have cheated anyone out of anything, I will pay it back four times over."

You see, that's what grateful faith does; it changes our lives. It changes what we put our trust in. Think about it like this. The words "In God We Trust" appear on our coins and on our paper money. The question is, "Do we trust in God?" or "Do we trust the money on which that motto is printed?"

In a nutshell, here's what happened to Zacchaeus that day in Jericho: He stopped trusting the money and started trusting God! He realized that day that discipleship is better than dollars. As Christians, we are rich in the things that count the most because, first of all, we are rich in God. We are rich in faith.

Second, There Is Church

The church is another of the riches of life that count the most. Zacchaeus had gotten tied in with the Romans and had gotten wealthy off the deal. But in the process, he had lost his church. Please don't let that happen to you. Stay close to the church. It's one of the most valuable gifts God has given us.

Now, let me say something to parents and grandparents with all the feeling I have in my heart. You can give your children cashmere sweaters or ski trips to Colorado or sports cars if you want. But let me tell you something. Without question, the best gift you can give them is Jesus Christ and his church. If you want to do something good for your children, if you want to give them the gift that keeps on giving, if you want to give them a gift that shows them how much you love them, then introduce them to Jesus Christ and his church. Get them completely involved in serving Christ through his church. It's the best gift you can give them, the most valuable thing that you can do for them.

Now, of course, we can't make that decision for them. Ultimately, it is a personal decision. But we can strongly encourage them in that direction, and that is our calling: to show them with words and actions how important the church is. I am so proud of our church and the incredible things we do that so powerfully touch the lives of people in the name of Christ.

Recently I went to a small civic committee luncheon at the Houston Club downtown. Just ten people were there. Only one person at that meeting was a member of St. Luke's, the church I pastored, but every single person there was being touched in some significant way by St. Luke's.

One woman was an educator, and she thanked me for St. Luke's because she said all of her in-service training was held there and our church always welcomed them so warmly and so graciously.

Another said her son attended our day school and loved it.

Another said her daughter came to St. Luke's to take piano lessons regularly.

On and on it went, all these people being touched by our church I felt so grateful and so gratified and so fortunate to be a part of our great church.

Recently, we had a new member party to rewelcome the new members who had joined the church in recent weeks. We asked the people there to tell us about themselves and what brought them to our church.

One young couple there that night fascinated me with what they said. The young wife's name is Dalia and she is from Mexico. Her husband's name is Christolf and he is from Germany. They come from different backgrounds, different countries, different cultures, and different denominations. They had been looking and looking for a church that was right for them. Dalia said, "When we walked into St. Luke's, the people were so kind, so gracious, the sanctuary so beautiful, the worship service so wonderful, and I knew," she said, "that God resides in this place. I could feel his presence, and it just felt like home." Christolf said, "That's right. When we came here we knew we were at home."

Isn't that beautiful? I was so proud of the church that I wanted to go get another commitment card and make another pledge to support it. As Christians, we are "rich in the things that count the most" because, first, we have faith. Second, we have the church.

Third and Finally, There Is Love

Zacchaeus became "rich" in a new way that day in Jericho because he learned from Jesus the power of love.

Some weeks ago, Mitzi Scott, who works with our children's choir program, Sunday Sing, told the children that her sister-in-law—who is a nurse and a major in the Air Force—had been sent to Iraq to work with a medical field unit in that dangerous war-torn area.

The children wanted to help, so first they sent cards to Mitzi's sister-in-law. She wrote thank-you notes and spoke of their needs there. The children responded. They started bringing candy, gum, tea, coffee, and hot chocolate mix to choir practice on Sunday night, and these items were sent to the medical mission station in Iraq. Then they sent plastic pillowcases and phone cards and cookies.

The major mentioned that in addition to helping those wounded in action there, they helped heal a nine-year-old girl who had been bitten by a viper. Word spread about that, and now mothers with tiny babies who need bottles and formula and diapers were showing up at the mission station. The major asked her supply officer to order supplies to set up a pediatric clinic. The supply officer said: "I can do it, Major, but it will take ninety days." The major said: "St. Luke's can beat that!" And we did!

She sent an e-mail, and the children of our church responded. Word spread through our church family about what the children were doing and others stepped up to help. The St. Cecilia Choir, the Chancel Choir, a Bible study group, the ushers—all came forward to help. And today there is a pediatric unit in a medical mission station in Iraq because our children are being taught in our church the beauty and power of Christlike service, Christlike compassion, and Christlike love.

The major has ordered a special flag that will soon be flown in Iraq. The flag has these words: "Thank you, St. Luke's United Methodist Church, Operation Iraqi Freedom."

Let me ask you something: Do you feel blessed? Do you feel rich— rich in the things that really matter, rich in the things that last?

As Christians, we are rich beyond measure because we have faith, we have the church, and we have love. Those are the things that count the most.

1

Rich in the Scriptures

What the Bible Teaches Us

Scripture: 2 Timothy 3:14-17

ON NOVEMBER 4, 1879, IN OOLOGAH INDIAN TERRITORY (what is now Oklahoma), a baby boy was born. He was the youngest of eight children. His name was Will Rogers (www.willrogers.org).

While growing up on the family ranch, Will Rogers worked with the cattle and learned to ride and lasso from a young age. He became so talented with a rope that he was placed in the *Guinness Book of World Records* for throwing three lassos at the same time: one went around the horse's neck, another circled the rider, and the third flew under the horse, looping all four legs together.

Will Rogers dropped out of school in the tenth grade and became a show business performer, first with a wild west show, then a circus, then vaudeville, and then the Ziegfeld Follies.

Will Rogers loved talking to people and reading; and these two interests groomed him to become a humorist. His intelligent and amusing observations about people, life, the country, and the government, expressed in simple down-home language that his audience could understand and relate to, caused people to love his humor even more than his roping tricks. He became a movie star, appeared in seventy-one films and several Broadway productions, and in 1934 was voted the most popular male actor in Hollywood. Then, Will Rogers's career took a different turn that endeared him to even more people. He became a writer. He wrote four thousand syndicated columns and six books and became a radio broadcaster and a political commentator. His folksy humor and honest, intelligent observations about life, the government, and America earned the respect of the nation.

Will Rogers died in a plane crash in 1935. And to this day, he is still regarded as the greatest political sage and humorist our country has ever known. Here are some of his famous quotes:

🐦 "Never slap a man who's chewing tobacco."

🐦 "Even if you're on the right track, you'll get run over if you just sit there."

🐦 "There are two theories to arguing with a woman; neither works."

🐦 "If you find yourself in a hole, stop digging."

🐦 "The quickest way to double your money is to fold it and put it back in your pocket."

🐦 "Live in such a way that you would not be ashamed to sell your parrot to the town gossip."

🐦 "Lettin' the cat out of the bag is a whole lot easier'n puttin' it back."

Wise sayings like these of Will Rogers have been with us since the beginning of time. They are a part of every language and every people's heritage. The Old Testament contains an entire book of proverbs, or wise sayings, and additional wisdom literature with fascinating sayings, which have been handed down from generation to generation. Sayings such as these:

🐦 A soft answer turns away wrath. (15:1)

🐦 The fear of the LORD is the beginning of knowledge. (1:7)

🐦 A good name is to be chosen rather than great riches. (22:1)

Also, some years before the time of Christ, Cicero was giving us some words that have been repeated millions of times since he first spoke them: "One does not have to believe everything he hears," and "Virtue is its own reward." And when we really stop to think about it, we see that the Ten Commandments were in a sense wise sayings that Moses and the early Israelites felt were worth repeating, worth saying again and again.

Now, with all this in mind, let's look closer at riches of the Bible. The Bible is full of wise sayings, strong commandments, great lessons, thoughtful parables, excellent examples, and powerful events that serve to teach us God's way, God's truth, God's will for us in this life.

Remember how the apostle Paul expressed it in his second letter to his close friend Timothy. He said, "But as for you, continue in what you have learned and firmly believed, knowing from whom you learned it, and how from childhood you have known the sacred writings that are able to instruct you for salvation through faith in Christ Jesus. All scripture is inspired by God and is useful for teaching, for reproof, for correction, and for training in righteousness, so that everyone who belongs to God may be proficient, equipped for every good work" (2 Timothy 3:14-17).

Recently, I had the privilege of giving Bibles to the third graders in our church. In anticipation of that significant event, I tried to think of how to express to our children, and all of us, in three simple sentences, or three wise sayings, what the Bible teaches us. And here's what I came up with. I'm sure that you will think of other ideas (there are so many), but for now look with me at these three basic sentences that remind us what the Bible teaches us.

First, the Bible Teaches Us to Love God Because He First Loves Us

Again and again, Jesus says this: God is a loving Father (not an angry, hostile, vengeful deity who must be appeased), a loving Father who cannot rest until he finds his lost children.

This is the recurring theme of Jesus' teaching and we see this especially in Luke 15 in the parables of the lost sheep, the lost coin, and the lost son.

Interestingly, there are three different kinds of lostness depicted here: (1) the coin is lost by accident through no fault of its own; (2) the sheep is lost from wandering off, drifting away, going off on its own; (3) the son loses himself on purpose. He willfully, arrogantly, and pridefully runs away to the far country. But, in each case, the search is intense and victorious. And when the lost is found, there is great joy and celebration. Over and over the Bible teaches us this. We see it especially in the teachings of Jesus, the seeking, gracious, forgiving love of God! We love God because he first loves us.

His name was Ray. He had come to ask me a favor. His daughter (who was sixteen years old) was a teenage runaway, and someone had seen her in Dallas. He wanted me to go to Dallas with him. So, we went to Dallas in search of her. All day, one place after another, we looked. I'll never forget the intensity in Ray's face, the sense of urgency, the conscientious, dedicated manner of the search, the hopefulness in his eyes as we went into arcades and discothèques and coffeehouses and teenage hangouts. "Maybe she'll be here," he would say. We looked and looked all day long and into the night, but we didn't find her that day.

On the trip back home, we rode along in disappointed silence. I'll never forget Ray's slumped shoulders and misty eyes, his agonizing unrest, because he was separated from his daughter. His child was lost, and he was heartsick. He wanted to find her and bring her home.

She surfaced a few days later in Washington, D.C. She had heard somehow that her dad was in Dallas looking for her urgently. She was touched by his love. She called Ray crying. She wanted to come home. Ray was on the first plane to go get her and bring her back.

I learned something of what God is like that day with Ray—something of what Jesus taught in his parables about God's seeking love. God is a loving Father who desperately wants his children back. He wants to find them and bring them home. Nowhere is this more powerfully expressed than on the Cross at Calvary. "God so loved the world that he gave his only Son, so that everyone who believes in him may not perish but may have eternal life" (John 3:16).

That's why we love God, because he first loves us. When we understand that and accept that and celebrate that, then we can't sit still; we want to thank him and serve him and love him back.

Some years ago, Karl Barth, the noted theologian, was on a speaking tour in the United States. A student said to him, "Dr. Barth, you are one of the greatest theologians of all time. You have written volumes and volumes of theology, but can you sum up your faith in a single sentence?" Dr. Barth said: "Jesus loves me this I know for the

Bible tells me so." That's number one: the Bible teaches us to love God because he first loves us.

Second, the Bible Teaches Us to Love Other People for God's Sake

Some years ago when we were living in Shreveport, Louisiana, a young man came down and joined the church at the end of our worship service one Sunday morning. His name was Tommy. He lived in a church-sponsored home just two blocks from the church. Tommy decided that I would be his friend, and we did indeed become good friends.

Tommy was quite a character. He had a sweet spirit, but he frightened some people because he looked different and talked really loud; and sometimes in his innocence, he would say embarrassing things or ask me embarrassing questions. He didn't mean to say things that most people would not say in public. He was curious and we were friends and he felt like he could ask me anything, and often he did ask me in the most public places in a booming voice.

He worked at a nearby hospital. He put the linens in the supply closets and could do his job well as long as nobody changed the routine. If the routine changed, however, he would become lost and confused and frustrated. If the door always opened toward him, no problem. But if someone changed the door so that it opened away from him, he could not figure that out. It would never occur to him to try it the other way. But Tommy was a good guy and a special child of God. He needed a friend, and I decided that I would be a friend to him.

Tommy's afternoon off work was Tuesday. He got off at 1:00 P.M., and he always came straight to my office. It was a standing appointment that he set. Every Tuesday afternoon at 1:15 he would show up at my office with pictures from a trip he had made with his parents, and he would show me his pictures.

Tommy's favorite thing to do was to sit in my chair behind my desk. He would pretend that he was the minister and that I had come to see him. He loved to sit in my chair and put his feet up on my desk and show me the pictures from his latest trip. His parents were well-to-do and took him to a lot of wonderful places.

Tommy and I had been friends for some five or six years when one day I heard that Walter Underwood had been elected bishop and that the church he had been serving (St. Luke's United Methodist Church in Houston, Texas) was open and that I was being considered along with many others to be appointed its minister. A few weeks later, the bishop called me to tell me that some folks from St. Luke's were coming to hear me preach the very next Sunday morning, and he said, "I want you to do three things: (1) don't tell anybody they are coming; (2) don't call attention to them in any way; and (3) preach a good sermon."

Well, I went to work on that sermon and when Sunday morning arrived, I was ready. After the 8:30 service, after everybody left the sanctuary, I was cleaning up the church and straightening things to get ready for the next service and looked up and saw this distinguished group of people walking down the aisle. I thought, "That's got to be the group from St. Luke's," and it was. We spoke, introduced ourselves, and one of them said, "We liked your sermon." I was surprised because I didn't even realize they had been there. I was expecting them in the 11:00 service. At least the pressure was off. So we just stood there having a nice visit, when all of a sudden, the sanctuary door flew open, and I heard somebody loudly call my name: "JIM!"

I recognized that booming voice—my worst nightmare. It was Tommy, just back from a trip to New Orleans. I was always glad to see Tommy, but not at that moment, because I had no idea what he was going to do or say as I was trying to put my best foot forward. He ran down the aisle and hugged me. I introduced him: "Tommy, these are some friends of mine from Houston. Have you ever been to Houston?" "Oh, yes," he said, "to the Astrodome and Astroworld and the Galleria. Once I got lost there, and my parents had to get the police to find me." Then he said, "Can I come and see you Tuesday like I always do at 1:15?"

"Sure."

"Can I sit at your desk and play like I'm the minister like I always do?"

"Absolutely. And Tommy, bring your pictures from your New Orleans trip and we'll look at them together."

While all this was going on, I was praying, "O God, please, please don't let Tommy say something embarrassing." Well, God must have heard my prayer because, amazingly, Tommy said, "Jim, I'll see you Tuesday, but now I'm going to get my seat on the front row and get ready for the worship service."

The St. Luke's group and I visited a while longer, and then they left. I breathed a sigh of relief. The next day, the bishop called me and said, "Jim, you must have done a good job because they liked you." And I thought, "I'm going to go home and frame that sermon!" But was I ever in for a surprise. Some weeks later, when I was sent to St. Luke's, I discovered that it wasn't my sermon at all. That group of people who came to hear me preach said, "Jim, do you know when we decided that we wanted you to be our minister?"

"Was it my sermon?" I asked.

"No," they said. "It was when Tommy came in!"

I learned a great lesson that day, namely this: The greatest sermons don't happen in a pulpit. They happen when we love other people. They happen when we love other people for God's sake. First, the Bible teaches us to love God because he first loves us. Second, the Bible teaches us to love other people for God's sake.

Third and Finally, the Bible Teaches Us to Love Life Because It's God's Gift to Us

Life is not an endurance test. It is a gift from God to be celebrated day in and day out. The scriptures put it like this: "This is the day that the LORD has made; let us rejoice and be glad in it" (Psalm 118:24). At home we have a plaque with these words: "Today is God's gift to us; that's why we call it the Present."

Fred Craddock tells about an old red mule with which his family used to plow their garden. The mule would often get out of the fence, and it was Fred's job to find the mule and bring him home. Fred was just a young boy at the time, and he would have to go through the woods and across an old family cemetery to find the old red mule. It was scary for Fred to go through the old cemetery, and on top of that, his mother would always say, "Make sure you don't step on graves. Graves are sacred ground, and don't step on the graves." And young Fred would protest because he couldn't tell where the graves were. The cemetery ground was level, the markers were leaning over, and pine needles covered the ground. He said: "Mama, I can't tell what part is sacred." His mother answered, "Well, I know it all looks the same. But if you'll just treat it all as sacred, you'll never miss" (Fred B. Craddock, *Craddock Stories* [St. Louis, Mo.: Chalice Press, 2001], 91).

What a great lesson that is! Wherever we are, whatever we are doing, if we will learn to treat it all as a sacred gift from God, then we'll never miss. We will do well in this life. This is what the Bible teaches us.

🕉 To love God because he first loves us.

🕉 To love other people for God's sake.

🕉 To love life because it's God's gift to us.

When we understand this and build our lives around these great biblical lessons, then we are rich in the things that count the most. We are rich in the scriptures.

2

Rich in Soul

The Signs of a Healthy Spirit

================

Scripture: 1 Corinthians 12:27-31

I F WE WERE TO BRING TOGETHER A BRILLIANT GROUP OF DOCTORS, psychologists, and sociologists, and if we were to ask them the question, "What are the signs of a healthy brain?" they would probably list three things:

🕉 connectedness

🕉 communication

🕉 caring

Think of that with me for just a few moments.

The first sign of a healthy brain is connectedness. A healthy brain is beautifully and amazingly connected to the rest of the body. It's the brain that signals to us how to respond in every situation. It's the brain that prompts and directs every part of the body so that we know how to live and think and move and react. The brain tells the foot where to step and where not to step. The brain tells the hand what to touch and what not to touch. The brain tells the mouth what to taste and what not to taste.

And if there is a disconnect, if the brain somehow gets disconnected from any other part of the body, then we have a big problem and an unhealthy situation.

Let me illustrate that. I have a doctor friend who was playing golf at a country club in Houston some years ago. He stood over his golf

9

ball, ready to hit his drive. Suddenly, as he looked at his golf ball, his vision became distorted. Abruptly, he turned to his friends and said, "Take me to the emergency room; I have a brain tumor." Because of his training as a doctor, he knew immediately that there was a disconnect between his brain and his eyes, and he knew immediately what that meant. He knew he had a problem. He knew that he had an unhealthy brain because the first sign of a healthy brain is connectedness.

The second sign of a healthy brain is communication. A healthy brain enables us to communicate well and sometimes eloquently what we are wanting, feeling, thinking, needing, and expecting.

For example, when a football player takes a hard blow to the head and a concussion is suspected, the first thing the team doctor will do is ask the player some simple questions such as: "Where are you?" "What is your name?" "What day is it?" If the player can't figure out and communicate the correct answers to those elementary questions, then the doctor knows that there is a problem with the brain, and that finding indicates strongly that this is an unhealthy situation—probably a brain concussion—because the player can't think straight and can't communicate.

The third sign of a healthy brain is caring. A person with a healthy brain is able to receive love and to pass love on to others.

About five years ago, we launched our Parenting Center here at St. Luke's and brought in a brilliant doctor from the Houston Medical Center to speak to parents and teachers of preschool children. This doctor had done extensive research on the effect of love on the development of the brain. The doctor put up on a screen two pictures side by side. The pictures depicted the brains of two small children. The brain on the left side of the screen was the brain of a healthy child who had been loved and cherished by his parents. All of his life, he had been held and rocked and patted. All of his life, he had been talked to and sung to and encouraged with words and acts of love. All of his life, every day of his life, he had been reminded and reassured and shown in numerous ways that he was loved and treasured and cared for.

The brain on the right side of the screen was the brain of an abused child, a neglected child, who was left alone in his crib all day long. No one fed him. No one talked to him, and no one held him. He was left all alone all day.

Now, don't miss this. The brain of the child who was cared for and loved and cherished was three times larger than the brain of the abused and neglected child! And there is a sermon there somewhere!

Connectedness, communication, and caring—these are the signs of a healthy brain. They are also the signs of a healthy church! Let me show you what I mean.

First of All, the First Sign of a Healthy Church Is Connectedness

The theme of our stewardship program a few years ago was "Get Connected." It was a great theme because a healthy, wholesome, vibrant church has a strong spirit of connectedness with God and with people. That's what it's all about—connecting with God and people.

Dr. Fred Craddock is one of the great preachers of our time. He tells a story about something that happened to him on an airplane some years ago. It was way back in the days when you could smoke on airplanes.

Dr. Craddock was on the flight to Denver, Colorado. He was seated in the no smoking section of the plane, as was his custom. Dr. Craddock was seated on the aisle. Just as they took off, directly across the aisle from Fred Craddock, a large tough-looking man pulled out a big cigar and lit it up and began to puff clouds of cigar smoke into the air. Dr. Craddock didn't want to cause a problem, but that cigar smoke was suffocating him. He decided to be discreet, so when the flight attendant came by, Fred Craddock stopped her.

In his words, she was a very, very attractive young woman. Dr. Craddock said to her, "Am I in the wrong section? I asked for no smoking." "This is no smoking," the flight attendant said. And just then she noticed the cigar smoke, so she turned to the man who was smoking and very politely told him that this was the no smoking section and he would have to extinguish his cigar. The man looked at her with hard eyes and just kept right on puffing that big cigar.

She went on down the aisle to attend to other matters. When she came back and saw that he was still smoking, she mentioned it to him again. He just took a big puff and blew cigar smoke in her face. A little later, the beautiful young flight attendant came back up the aisle. She was carrying a tray full of soft drinks. Just as she got to the spot directly between Fred Craddock and the cigar-smoking man, the plane hit some turbulence. The flight attendant went over with those soft drinks, and they all spilled, first on the man's cigar and then into his lap. Then, the plane hit another air pocket, and would you believe it? The beautiful young flight attendant lost her balance and fell right into Fred Craddock's lap! Dr. Craddock said, "Now, don't tell me there's no God. Once in a while you have an experience where you say, *Now, it's so obvious.* God really shouted there"(Fred B. Craddock, *Craddock Stories* [St. Louis, Mo.: Chalice Press, 2001], 39-40).

Now, let me ask you a very personal question: Do you know there is a God? And are you connected to him? At its best, this is what the church does—it connects people to God! At its best it becomes the conduit through which God reaches out to touch people with his amazing grace, his redemptive love, and his saving power. At its best, the church becomes our hearing aid, enabling us to tune in and hear the voice of God, the call of God, the will of God.

Also, at its best, the church helps us connect with one another. This is what the apostle Paul meant when he said, "We are the Body of Christ . . . members one of another, connected together in every way . . . and connected strongly to God" (paraphrase of Romans 12:4-5).

When we say "the church is the Body of Christ," what does that mean? It means that we are the continuators of Christ's ministry, and this is precisely why Christ came into our world—to connect us to God and to one another. Let me ask you something: Are you as closely connected to God and to other people as you could be or should be? If not, come to church. Get more involved in the life of the church. This is the place, this is the community of faith that can help you feel connected to God, to life, and to other people. That's why we need to be in church every Sunday. That's why we need to make church attendance a priority in our lives. It's the best way I know of to stay connected to God and to other people.

The Second Sign of a Healthy Church Is Communication

This means communication with God through prayer and worship and Bible study and service projects—all the Holy Habits—and communication with each other through words and hugs and acts of love. How crucial communication is in the life of the church! But sometimes communication is difficult. Let me show you what I mean.

A couple of weekends ago, I flew to Salina, Kansas, to speak at the installation event for the new bishop of Kansas. The committee orchestrating the significant experience had planned a full weekend of activities: a concert on Friday night; my speaking twice on Saturday morning, and then a formal service of installation of the bishop on Saturday afternoon.

I arrived at the hotel in Salina, Kansas, at 6:30 Friday night, just as everyone was leaving for the concert. I encouraged my hosts to go on to the concert; I would check into the hotel, get a bite to eat, and join them at the concert a little later. I checked in and discovered that the hotel was very nice, but it had no restaurant. But then I noticed about a hundred yards up in front of the hotel was a steak house, so I walked there to get dinner.

The place was packed. It was Friday night, and folks were everywhere waiting to get in and get a table. The hostess said, "How many?" And I said, "One, just me." She said, "You're by yourself?" "Yes," I said. Then she said, "I'll tell you what. It's going to be a long time before we can open up a table for one—forty-five minutes to an hour—but if you don't mind eating at the bar, you can be seated right now and order immediately."

Now, let me digress to tell you that I am an absolute teetotaler. I've never had a drink of alcohol of any kind in my life. The most dangerous thing I've ever passed over these lips is cherry-flavored soda!

I looked up at the bar, and it was completely empty. Right above the bar, the Houston Astros were playing on television, so I decided to go for it. The hostess smiled and seated me at the bar. I ordered my meal and started watching the Astros. Then I thought, I have got to tell June (my wife) about this. She was in Tennessee that night helping her mother recover from recent surgery.

I pulled out my cell phone and called her and said, "You will never believe what I'm doing right now. I'm in Salina, Kansas, and I have 'bellied up to the bar.'" I went on to explain, and we had a good laugh.

The next night I went back to that same restaurant and the situation was exactly the same. So in order to get my meal quickly, I went back to the bar again and ordered. This time Kansas and Texas Tech were playing football on TV. As I watched the game and waited for my meal, I laid my cell phone up on the bar. Almost immediately it rang, and I thought, *Oh, that's June calling.* I picked up the phone and said, "Well, I'm bellied up to the bar again." There was a long pause, and then I heard a voice say, "Dad, is that you?" It was our son Jeff calling. I had a hard time explaining why I had said what I had just said. Sometimes communication is difficult, especially if you don't know the context.

But put that over against this. Last weekend my wife, June, and I were having breakfast with our daughter, Jodi, and her family when suddenly June said this (I'm going to quote her precisely): "You know, this morning when I first woke up, I was thinking about . . ." and Jodi said, "I know it, Mom. I was thinking about that, too." June didn't even finish the sentence and Jodi knew what she was thinking about, knew what she was going to say. That happens all the time! They can finish each other's sentences!

I asked Jodi about that: "Jodi, how did you know what your mom was going to say?" I loved her answer. She said, "Daddy, she's my mother!" Isn't that beautiful? She is so connected to her mom that she just knows. She knows what she's gong to say before she even says it. She knows because she's tuned in to her mom. That is connectedness and communication at their very best!

The point is, if we live with somebody in a loving, trusting relationship over a period of time, we begin to think like that person thinks. If we spend enough quality time with Christ, we take on "the mind of Christ." In my opinion, the best way to do that is to get involved in the life of the church. It's always been true, and that's why when we join the church, we make that promise to God to support the church with our prayers, our gifts, our service, our presence, and our attendance! Being in church regularly helps keep us connected to God and to one another, and it keeps us in close communication with God and with one another. First, there is connectedness; second, communication.

The Third Sign of a Healthy Church Is Caring

It's that special spirit of receiving God's love and passing it on to others. When we in the church do that, that's when we are most powerfully the church.

A woman was asked by a coworker, "What's it like to be a Christian?" The woman replied, "It's like being a pumpkin. God picks you from the patch, brings you in, and washes all the dirt off of you. Then he reaches inside you and scoops out all the yucky stuff. He removes the seeds of selfishness and greed and prejudice and hate and pettiness. And then he carves you a new smiling face. And finally he puts his light of love inside of you to shine for all the world to see." That's our job as a church—to share the light of Christ and the love of God with the world.

If we are going to be a healthy church, then we need connectedness and communication and caring. Because, you see

🐚 a healthy church is connected tightly to God and to people;

🐚 a healthy church communicates well with God and with each other;

🐚 and most important, a healthy church reaches out to share God's love and care with everybody we meet.

If you want to help us do that then

Come to church!
Come to church every Sunday!
Make church attendance a real priority in your life!
Let God, through the instrument of the church, enrich your soul.

3

Rich in Church

What I Love about the Church

Scripture: Matthew 7:24-28

In 1972, OUR FAMILY MOVED FROM TENNESSEE TO SHREVEPORT, Louisiana. Now, this created an interesting problem for us because the people of Louisiana we encountered automatically thought that since we were from Tennessee we must be hillbillies. But we really weren't hillbillies, because we came from the Memphis area, which is not hill country at all.

And then when we would go back to Tennessee to visit our family there, the people of Tennessee automatically assumed that we were Louisiana Cajuns, which we really weren't, because we were living in Shreveport, which is in northwest Louisiana and is not in Cajun country at all.

But it brings to mind the time a Louisiana Cajun and a Tennessee hillbilly met on a narrow path. The Tennessee hillbilly was carrying a basket. The Louisiana Cajun said, "Whatcha got in that basket?" The Tennessee hillbilly said, "Fish." And the Louisiana Cajun said, "If I guess how many fish you've got in that basket, will you give me one of them?" The Tennessee hillbilly said, "If you guess how many fish I've got in this basket, I'll give you **both** of them." And the Louisiana Cajun said, "Five." And the Tennessee hillbilly said, "You missed it by two."

Now, we don't have to worry about any of that anymore, because one of the great dreams of life has come true for us—we are Texans and have been for the last twenty years and hope to be for the rest of our lives! But, you know, over the years, everywhere we have lived, we have learned fresh, new, and exciting ways to love the church!

Our early love for the church was born in Tennessee, and it was nurtured there. Then we spent twelve years in Shreveport, Louisiana, and there we learned even more about being servants of Christ and his church. And then on September 1, 1984, we came to Houston, Texas, to St. Luke's United Methodist Church. We are absolutely amazed, marvelously touched, and incredibly grateful for what our experiences there have taught us about what it means (and how special it is) to be a church family. Our church has accepted us, embraced us, and included us in so many sacred and precious moments.

Our church has loved us and encouraged us and inspired us. And in recent months, our church has comforted us and strengthened us as we have shared the joys and sorrows and challenges of life together. Our church has taught us so much, and now we find ourselves loving the church more than ever, loving God and the church family more than words could ever express. So, with this in mind, I don't want to be overly emotional or too sentimental, but I would like to be very personal with you. I simply want to share with you what I love about the church.

I could write a book on this because there are so many things I love about the church—I am so indebted to the church. Over the years, God, through the church, has given me

🕭 a wonderful upbringing

🕭 a good education

🕭 a relevant theology

🕭 a terrific family

🕭 a sense of purpose and mission and meaning

🕭 a calling to ministry

🕭 a great opportunity to see the world

🕭 a great place to celebrate life

🕭 and a great community in which to serve Christ and to proclaim his good news.

I could write a book on each one of those. But right now, I want to focus on three other things I love about the church. I'm sure you will think of others, but for now let's look together at these three.

First of All, I Love the Church Because the Church Introduced Me to the Christian Lifestyle

The church taught me that it is just not enough to "talk a good game." We are called to *live* our faith daily. Christianity is not just a creed we profess; it is a lifestyle. It affects the way we act, the way we think, the way we speak, the way we work, the way we live, the way we respond to life, and the way we treat other people.

A few months ago, a letter arrived at the church for one of our staff members. The staff member has given me permission to share the letter, but has asked (for modesty's sake) that I not use his name or the letter-writer's name. It reads like this:

Dear —

I am not a member of your church and we have not been formally introduced. However, I have seen you and your wife eating at the taqueria in town. On one occasion this spring, you showed an interest in my five-year old son, David. Your kindness and tenderness truly touched my heart.

When we saw you at the restaurant, David was scheduled to have his third heart surgery. He was born with multiple heart defects, and given the complexity of those defects, his survival was uncertain. In fact, his cardiologist said David would have a 60 percent chance of living to the age of fifteen if he lived long enough to receive all of his needed surgeries.

When you showed an interest in David that day, I felt that God was demonstrating to me that He was watching over my son. David had that surgery in May and although there were complications, he made a complete recovery and his prognosis is excellent. David is enjoying a healthy and normal childhood.

Sometimes when a parent has worried about his child for so many years, it is wonderful to feel God's love and support through another's act of kindness.

With great gratitude . . .

That letter touched me deep down in my soul because that's what it's all about. It's about living our faith every moment out there in the world! That's what we advocate strongly in our church. That's what we want every member of our church family to do—to reach out to others in the loving spirit of Christ. That's what our church's mission statement means: "St. Luke's is a Christ-centered servant church where every member is a minister."

Edgar Guest once put it like this in his poem "Sermons We See":

I'd rather see a sermon than hear one any day;
I'd rather one should walk with me than merely tell
the way.

That's why I love the church: because the church introduced me to the Christian lifestyle.

Second, I Love the Church Because the Church Introduced Me to the Power of Hope

I wish you could talk to my wife, June's, mother today. Her name is Mildred Daniels. She lives in Tennessee. On her next birthday she will be eighty-eight years old. If you had talked to her on the telephone a few months ago and then talked to her today, you would think she is a different person.

In July (and for many months before) she was in constant pain. She needed a hip replacement, but some of her doctors were concerned that she was not strong enough to withstand the surgery. She was told that very soon she would not be able to walk, would be bedridden, and would have to move into a nursing home. She was blue and blah, and you could hear it in her voice. She sounded so down. But then we found one of the best surgeons in west Tennessee, and Mrs. Daniels went to see him, but without much hope. I told June that I just wanted the surgeon to be definitive, not wishy-washy, and here's what he said: "Mrs. Daniels, you have a choice. You can choose not to have this surgery and pretty soon you won't be able to walk, you will be confined to bed, and you will be in pain every day. Or, you can have this surgery and soon you will be able to walk, and you won't be in pain. If you were my mother, I would say, 'Let's go do the surgery today!'"

Well, that was about as definitive as you can get. She had the surgery in August and is doing great. Now she has a lilt in her voice that hasn't been there for a long time. Why? Of course, it's because she had successful surgery. Of course, it's because she is not in pain, but more, even more, it's because her hope has been restored. She now has something to look forward to.

She will be able to walk. She will be able to sleep. She will be able to drive her car. She will be able to go into the kitchen and cook (which she loves to do). Her life has been turned around and changed because of the power of hope.

This is one of the greatest things about the church—the message of hope, the promise that because of God we always have something to look forward to.

This is the great assurance of the Bible, the power of hope that nothing (not even death) can separate us from God and his love, that whatever we have to face in this life and the next, God will be there for us.

Last Tuesday, Reverend John Price came to our church to speak to the United Methodist Women on near-death experiences. He has been a hospital chaplain for some years and has kept a journal of eighty-nine patients who have had near-death experiences. These patients talk about bright lights, out-of-body experiences, and the feeling of peace and serenity. All of these were fascinating, he said, but one was stunning!

One Sunday morning, he baptized a baby girl who was just seven weeks old. The very next day, the mother of the little girl was feeding her infant daughter when the baby went totally limp, with no signs of life at all. The mom screamed for her husband and started mouth-to-mouth resuscitation. They rushed to the emergency room of the hospital where the baby girl had been born just seven weeks before. The ER staff did a great job; they got her breathing again. The next day, her parents took her home healthy as could be.

Four years later, the little girl and her mom drove by that hospital. The little girl, now four years old, pointed to the hospital and said, "Look, Mommy, look! That's where Jesus came to get me and brought me back!" The mother was stunned by that. She pulled her car over to the side of the road and said to the little girl, "What did you say?" And the little girl said it again: "That building! That's where Jesus came to get me and brought me back!"

Now, here's the amazing part. That family had never told the little girl about her near-death experience when she was seven weeks old. That family had not been back inside a church since the day of the baby's baptism. That family had never mentioned the name of Jesus to their little girl. They didn't go to church or Sunday school or do anything spiritual back then. But let me tell you something, they do now! That day when that little girl pointed at that hospital and said, "That's where Jesus came to get me and brought me back," that day changed their lives and brought them back to the church.

Now, I can't explain that scientifically. I don't know how a four-year-old girl could remember something that happened to her when she was a seven-week-old baby, except to say, "With God, all things are possible." But I do know one thing: This dramatic story reminds us of God's great promise that in this life—and in the life to come—he will be there to watch over us and take care of us. That is our hope!

That's the good news of our Christian faith and that's why I love the church. I love the church because the church introduced me, first, to the Christian lifestyle and, second, to the power of hope.

Third and Finally, I Love the Church Because the Church Introduced Me to Jesus

That's the bottom line, isn't it? We in the church exist to share Jesus Christ with a needy world, to introduce people to him. And everything we do is for that purpose. We have worship services, Sunday school classes, prayer groups, support groups, Bible study groups, youth groups, children's groups, singles' groups, senior groups, and mission work groups. We take trips, play games, present concerts, paint houses, build clinics, feed the hungry, and help the needy all for one purpose: so we can share the love of Jesus Christ, so we can tell people about him and his power to help us and save us and heal us.

Last May, Methodist Hospital here in Houston dedicated a majestic and beautiful new piece of sculpture in the main lobby of the hospital. It was placed there in loving memory of our St. Luke's member Randy Smith. Perfectly positioned and wonderfully lit, the statue dramatically depicts a woman kneeling before Jesus. Jesus is reaching out to the woman, tenderly touching her head and healing her.

Every time June and I have gone to the hospital for her chemotherapy, she goes first to that statue. We touch the statue and have a prayer before her treatment. June says she imagines that she is that woman kneeling before Jesus and that he is reaching out to touch and heal her.

That's a great image because that is indeed the way it works. We kneel before Christ with whatever ails us, with whatever our need may be. It may be a physical problem or an emotional problem or a spiritual problem. Whatever it is, we can bring it to Jesus Christ, and he can give us the healing we need because he is the Great Physician.

That's the good news of our Christian faith and that's why I love the church. The church introduced me, first, to the Christian lifestyle; second, to the power of hope; and third and most important of all, to Jesus. When you have these three in your life, you are rich, indeed—rich in the things that count the most.

4

Rich in the Power of
Life-Changing Words

The Sacred Power of Words

Scripture: Psalm 19:7-14

EVERY NOW AND THEN, I RUN ACROSS A LIST OF CHURCH BULLETIN bloopers. Let me share just a few of these with you:

🕭 Ladies, don't forget the rummage sale. It's a chance to get rid of those things not worth keeping around the house anymore. Don't forget your husbands.

🕭 Next Thursday, there will be tryouts for the choir. Please come. They need all the help they can get.

🕭 Barbara remains in the hospital and needs blood donors. She is also having trouble sleeping and requests tapes of Pastor Josh's sermons.

🕭 The Pastor will preach his farewell sermon, after which the choir will sing "Break Forth into Joy."

🕭 Irving Benson and Jessie Carter were married last Saturday. So ends a friendship that began in school days.

🕭 The Low Self-Esteem Support Group will meet Thursday at 7:00 P.M. Please use the back door.

Well, the point is clear: the words we use and the ways in which we communicate them are so important. Let me show you what I mean.

Some years ago at a football game in Southern California, a doctor at a first aid station found himself suddenly treating four patients for stomach disorders. Each patient had nausea, dizziness, and cramps, which are symptoms of food poisoning.

The doctor did a little detective work and discovered that all four of the patients had bought soft drinks at the stadium concession stand. Wanting to protect the rest of the crowd just in case the problem might have been caused by faulty soft drinks, an announcement was made over the stadium public address system, telling the fans that it would be wise to avoid the soft drinks because four people had become quite ill, possibly from the soft drinks.

The immediate effect of the announcement was amazing. The stadium became an arena of fainting and retching people. One hundred and ninety-one persons had to be hospitalized. Ambulances and private cars rushed people to the hospital, where emergency room doctors reported that the symptoms of food poisoning were genuine and dramatic.

Further questioning, however, revealed that all four of the original patients had eaten potato salad from the same delicatessen on the way to the game. The potato salad, not the soft drinks, was the culprit. Word was spread, and suddenly those who had been so sick immediately began to feel better. Before long, all of the 191 patients had recovered completely! (Norman Cousins, *The Healing Heart: Antidotes to Panic and Helplessness* [New York: W. W. Norton & Co., 1983].)

There's a sermon there somewhere, and it has to do with the power of words and the sacred responsibility that is ours in the choice, the content, the use, and the tone of our words. Words have such incredible power, probably more power than we even realize.

🕊 Words can build up or tear down.

🕊 Words can lift and inspire or crush and kill.

🕊 Words can bring harmony or breed suspicion.

🕊 Words can offer a beautiful prayer or incite an ugly riot.

🕊 Words can give a great message or tell a dirty joke.

Words are so powerful, so influential, so important. When God created the world, he spoke it into existence. He said, "Let there be light: and there was light" (Genesis 1:3 KJV) A lot of things get spoken into existence. That's why before every sermon I preach, I offer a special prayer that is a paraphrase of our text, Psalm 19:14: "Let the words of my mouth and the meditations of [our hearts] be acceptable in your sight, O Lord, [our] strength, and [our] redeemer" (KJV).

It is so important what we say, what we put into words, because words are so powerful, so awesome, so life-changing. Let me show you what I mean.

First, Our Words Need to Be Acceptable to God Because Words Can Change People Physically

The noted writer Norman Cousins speaks about this in his book, *The Healing Heart.* He gives a dramatic personal illustration of how words can change people physically. He says:

> In the fall of 1982, I saw an ambulance in front of the clubhouse of one of the golf courses in West Los Angeles. I went over to the ambulance and saw a man on a stretcher alongside the vehicle. He had suffered a heart attack while playing golf. The paramedics [were] working systematically and methodically.
>
> No one was talking to the man. He was ashen and trembling. . . . [The cardiograph monitor] revealed . . . a runaway heart rate. . . .
>
> I put my hand on his shoulder. "Sir," I said, "you've got a great heart."
>
> He opened his eyes and turned toward me. "Why do you say that?" he asked in a low voice.
>
> In Oliver Wendell Holmes's phrase, I "rounded the sharp corners of the truth" with my reply.
>
> "Sir," I said, "I've been looking at your cardiograph and I can see that you're going to be all right. You're in very good hands. In a few minutes, you'll be in one of the world's best hospitals. You're going to be just fine."
>
> "Are you sure?" he asked.
>
> "Certainly . . . Don't worry. You'll be all right."
>
> In less than a minute, the cardiograph showed . . . a slowing down of the heartbeat. . . . The rhythm began to be less irregular. I looked at the man's face; the color began to return. He propped

27

up his head with his arms and looked around; he was taking an interest in what was happening.

I felt no remorse at having skirted around the truth. What he needed—as much as the oxygen—was reassurance. (pp. 203-4)

Here we have a dramatic example of the power of words, a vivid reminder of how our words can change people physically. So, the lesson is obvious: we need to be very careful about what we say to people. Our words need to be gracious and kind and loving to people and acceptable to God.

Second, Our Words Need to Be Acceptable to God Because They Can Change People Emotionally

With our words, we can lift the emotions of people, or we can knock the life out of them. With our words, we can pick people up, or we can absolutely flatten them.

Now, let me ask you something. Have you ever had one of those days? Have you ever had a day when everything seemed to go wrong and everybody you met that day was upset about something and they were all taking it out on you? Most of the time (99.99 percent of the time), I am a happy, positive, upbeat, optimistic person. But every now and then, I have one of those days. Let me tell you about one I had some years ago.

I was so tired that I overslept. Then in my rush to get going that morning, as I hurriedly bent over to tie my shoes, my back went out. Then, walking to protect my aching back, my problematic left knee puffed up. On the way to work, I stopped by the bank to see how much money I had in my account, and the teller said she could tell me, but she would have to charge me ten dollars for that information. (That went over real well.) Then, between the bank and my office several blocks away, I ran out of gas and had to walk to work with a sore back and a swollen knee.

When I finally made it to the church, all day long, one right after another, and often several at a time, there were problems, problems, and more problems. This was very unusual for St. Luke's because most of the time (99.99 percent of the time), everybody is happy and gracious and positive, and everything is beautiful. But on this day, the moon must have been out of whack because everybody I saw was upset. They all had problems, and they were all bringing their problems to me and wanting me to fix their problems right now.

It was a horrible day. My back hurt. My knee hurt. My feelings were hurt. I had not had anything to eat all day. I was discouraged, disillusioned, down, tired, hungry. I thought to myself: *This is enough to make Norman Vincent Peale a pessimist!*

Finally, at about 6:00 that evening, I got to my mail. At the bottom of the stack was a personal letter with words I will never forget, words that turned my day around. It read in part like this:

> Dear Jim,
>
> If you ever have one of those days when you wonder, "Am I doing any good? Is it worth it? Does anybody care?" I hope you will remember this letter.
>
> If you ever have one of those days when you feel tired and discouraged and disillusioned, I hope you will remember this letter.
>
> If you ever have one of those days when you are tempted to quit and throw in the towel, I hope you will pull out this letter and read it again because you need to know that God, through you and St. Luke's, saved my life, redeemed my life, and turned my life around. There are no words big enough to tell you what this church has done for me!
>
> So, if you ever have one of those days, I hope you will remember me and I hope you will remember my letter.

I will always remember that letter because it came at a moment when I needed it so much, and those words inspired me to hitch up my belt and try again. The power of words can lift our emotions. The power of words can change people physically and emotionally.

Third and Finally, Our Words Need to Be Acceptable to God Because Words Can Change People Spiritually

One of Fred Craddock's most famous stories is a true story that took place years ago. A missionary family had served in China for some time when suddenly one day Communist soldiers barged into their home and placed them under house arrest. They had been prisoners in their own home for some sixty days when one morning, the soldiers came to the missionary (whose name was Glen) and told him and his wife that they would be released and flown to freedom the next morning, but that they could only take two hundred additional pounds with them.

Now, they had been in China for many years, and they had accumulated many things, so hard decisions would have to be made quickly. Only two hundred additional pounds. They began discussing what to take. Glen said, "Of course, we must take all of my books and sermons and my new typewriter." "Oh, Glen," answered his wife, "your books weigh so much, and you don't need to take the typewriter. Besides, I have my antique vases. They are so special, we must take them."

What started as a nice discussion soon became a full-scale heated argument. Each thought the other was being selfish and stubborn. Each was praying that God would bring the other to his or her senses. They went to bed that night in angry silence, neither of them willing to bend even a little or give an inch.

The next morning when the soldiers arrived with their scales, Glen elbowed in ahead of his wife and hurriedly placed his books, his sermons, and his typewriter on the scales. His wife stood to the side hugging her antique vases and seething.

The soldiers weighed Glen's belongings and said, "They weigh two hundred pounds."

"That's what you said," answered Glen, "Two hundred pounds."

"Yes, that's right," said the soldiers, "but how much do the children weigh?"

"You mean?"

"Yes! Yes!"

With tears of shame in his eyes, Glen laid his books and sermons and typewriter aside. He looked over to see his wife putting down her antique vases. Then they ran into each other's arms, holding each other tightly, hugging each other, and saying, "How could we have been so foolish? God forgive us!" (Fred Craddock, *Craddock Stories* [St. Louis, Mo.: Chalice Press, 2001], 22-23).

Those words, "How much do the children weigh?" brought them

to their senses, brought them back to their priorities, brought them back to each other and back to God.

Oh, the power of words! Words have the power to change people physically, emotionally, and spiritually. Oh, the power of words! Oh, the sacred power of words! The right words at the right time. They are rich with the power to change lives.

5

Rich in Christian Freedom

Trapped in a Prison of Our Own Making

Scripture: Mark 10:17-22

RECENTLY I READ A STORY ABOUT A MAN WHO BECAME AGITATED ABOUT the price of eggs. So, he decided to do something about it. He decided that he would raise his own chickens. He went to the store and bought all the supplies he would need to build a pen for his chickens—chicken wire, two-by-fours, posts, and metal stakes—and he began building a pen.

When it was completed, he stepped back to admire his work. It was a great job. He was really proud of himself until he suddenly realized that he had made one big mistake. He had trapped himself inside the pen! He was trapped in a prison of his own making!

Many of us can hear that story and honestly say, "Been there, done that. Got the T-shirt!" Is that man's experience with his self made prison a parable for us? Do we have fears or attitudes or problems or weaknesses that imprison us? Do we have crippling phobias or anxieties or worries that cut us off from life, from other people, or from God? Are we free to live life fully, with joy and excitement and enthusiasm as God intended? Or are we trapped in a prison of our own making?

Listen to these poignant words written by a teenager:

> I want to touch you world
> But I don't want to leave my shell,
> (Wilson Weldon, *Breakthru*
> [Nashville: Upper Room, 1972], p. 53)

33

Here we see it: the longing of a young person to touch the world, to taste life, but afraid of the risks, the demands, the responsibilities.

Does that sound familiar to you? It does to me. It reminds me of something I've felt personally. It reminds me of something I've seen in others. And it reminds me of something in the Bible.

In the tenth chapter of Mark's Gospel, the story of Christ's encounter with the rich young ruler speaks to this dramatically. Remember it with me. Jesus is on his way to Jerusalem, on his way to the cross, when the rich young ruler runs up and kneels before Christ. Notice this: *He runs up* (a sign of enthusiasm), and *he kneels* (a sign of respect and reverence).

Thus, we can assume here that this young man is not trying to trap Jesus with a loaded question (as others tried), but that he is really sincere when he asks, "Good Teacher, what must I do to inherit eternal life?" Jesus answers, "You know the commandments: 'Do not kill, Do not commit adultery, Do not steal, Do not bear false witness, Do not defraud, Honor your father and mother.'" Then the young man answers, "All these I have observed from my youth." Jesus then looks at him with love and says to him, "You lack one thing; go, sell what you have, and give to the poor, and you will have treasure in heaven; and come, follow me" (RSV).

At this, the rich young ruler turns away and leaves sorrowfully, trapped in a prison of his own making, trapped by his own fears and attitudes.

Let me ask you something. Are you trapped like that? Are you trapped in a prison of your own making? Many people are. Let me show you what I mean with three thoughts.

First of All, We Can Get Trapped in a Prison of Mixed-Up Priorities

We can major in minors. As my college speech teacher used to say, we can make the mistake of putting the em-PHA-sis on the wrong syl-LA-ble. We can get all excited and all perturbed about the things that don't really matter that much and miss the true treasures of life.

This was in part the rich young ruler's problem. He was so caught up in material things, in living the material life, that he turned and walked away from the real life, the abundant life, the eternal life he could have had in Jesus Christ. He had lots of questions about lots of things, but he was not able to make the leap of faith.

Fred Craddock is one of the great preachers in America today. He tells about something that happened to him when he was twenty years old. He read Albert Schweitzer's book, *The Quest for the Historical Jesus*. Dr. Craddock said he was a young theology student and when he read the book, he had lots of questions that he realized later smacked of sophomoric enthusiasm and youthful arrogance. "This Christology is woeful material. It is more water than wine," he thought as he read Schweitzer's words.

As he read through the book, he marked it up, crossing out whole paragraphs and putting big question marks in the margins. He said that he was extremely critical and harsh in his judgments of Albert Schweitzer's writing. Not long after he read the book, he heard that Albert Schweitzer was coming to America. He was coming to play a dedicatory concert on a new organ in a big church in Cleveland, Ohio. Remember that Schweitzer was a philosopher, a theologian, a medical doctor, a pastor, and a world-class concert organist.

Fred Craddock was in Knoxville, Tennessee, at the time. He bought a ticket on the Greyhound bus to go from Knoxville to Cleveland. He said that all the time he was on the bus making that long trip, he had Dr. Schweitzer's book out and was going over his notes again, and he was writing down questions to ask Albert Schweitzer. He was really going to interrogate Dr. Schweitzer and hold his feet to the fire. Beside each of his questions, he wrote down the page references so that when he had the chance to talk with Dr. Schweitzer, he could say, "On page so-and-so, you said this, and I don't believe it. On page so-and-so, you said this and that contradicts the other." He was ready to straighten out Albert Schweitzer.

Fred Craddock made it to Cleveland, went to the concert, and was mesmerized by Schweitzer's brilliant performance on the new church organ. When the concert was over, Fred Craddock ran to the fellowship hall and sat down in the front row because the announcement had said that there would be a time of refreshments and fellowship afterward. Fred Craddock was all set. He had all of his tough, academic, theological questions laid out in his lap.

Finally, Albert Schweitzer walked in. He had shaggy hair and a big mustache. He was stooped over, seventy-five years of age at the time. He was carrying a little cup of tea and a small plate with a couple of goodies on it. Schweitzer walked to the microphone in the front of the room and said, "You've been very warm, hospitable to me. I thank you for it, and I wish I could stay longer, but I must go back to Africa. I must go back to Africa because my people are poor and diseased and hungry and dying, and I have to go. We have a medical station at Lambarene. If there's anyone here in this room who has the love of Jesus, would you be prompted by that love to go with me and help me?"

Fred Craddock said that at that moment he looked at the questions in his lap and they were all utterly stupid. He said, "And I learned, again, what it means to be Christian and had hopes that I could be that someday" (Fred Craddock, *Craddock Stories* [St. Louis, Mo.: Chalice Press, 2001], 125-26).

The point is clear: when Jesus calls us, he doesn't question us about our theology, he doesn't question us about our academic accomplishments. He is just interested in our answer to one question: Will you follow me? Will you serve with me? Will you help me take care of those who are sick and lonely and hurting? Will you join forces with me in reaching out to help the needy?

The rich young ruler turned away sorrowfully that day because he was trapped in a prison of his own making, a prison of mixed-up priorities. Sometimes that happens to us. We can get so focused on matters that don't matter that we miss the one thing in life that really does matter, and that is indeed sorrowful.

Second, We Can Get Trapped in a Prison of Pride

Now, of course, we know that there is a good kind of pride. We should be proud of our children and especially proud of our grandchildren! We should be proud of our church and our city and our nation. But that's not the kind of pride that's the problem here. Rather, it's that brand of pride that makes people arrogant and haughty and hypocritical, the kind of pride that is the opposite of humility.

The rich young ruler may well have wanted to follow Jesus that day, but his pride imprisoned him. "I'm a big man, an important man, a respected man in this community. I'm a rich young ruler! What will people say if I follow this lowly carpenter, this itinerant preacher from Nazareth. What will people think?" That kind of pride can come back to haunt us.

Have you heard the story about the woman who was to bake a cake for the church ladies' bake sale but forgot to do it until the last minute? Alice was her name. She baked an angel food cake. But when she took it out of the oven, the center had dropped flat. It was too late to bake another cake, so she looked around the house for something to build up the center of the cake. Alice found it in the bathroom—a roll of toilet paper. She plunked it in and covered it with beautiful, luscious icing. The finished product looked elegant and sumptuous, so she rushed it to the church.

Alice then gave her daughter some money and asked her to be at the bake sale the minute the doors opened and buy the cake and bring it straight home. But when the daughter arrived at the bake sale, the attractive cake had already been sold. Alice was beside herself.

A couple of days later, Alice was invited to a friend's home for a festive party. A fancy lunch was served, and to top it off, the cake in question was presented for dessert. When Alice saw the notorious cake, she started to get out of her chair to rush into the kitchen to tell her hostess all about it. But before she could get to her feet, one of the other ladies said, "What a beautiful cake!" to which the hostess said, "Thank you; I baked it myself!" At this point, Alice sat back in her chair just to watch what would happen next!

Well, there's a sermon there somewhere, and it's about how our mixed-up priorities and our haughty pride can come back to haunt us, and when that happens, it is indeed sorrowful.

Third and Finally, We Can Get Trapped in a Prison of Half-Heartedness

When I was in high school, I spent the weekend with a buddy of mine. He was Catholic, and I was interested in going to church with him because I had never been to a Catholic church before. I wanted to see what that was like. We planned to go to his church and then head to the lake. When we got to his church, we parked and then went to the front door. "Come on. This won't take long. Just do what I do," he said.

We stepped into the narthex of the church, and that's as far as we got. My friend went over, dipped his hand into the holy water, and crossed himself. He motioned for me to do the same. I did, and then we headed back out of the church, ran to the car laughing, and sped off to the lake. That was our experience of church that day: it took all of thirty seconds.

I have thought of that experience often. It's a vivid parable for our time because every church has a similar problem. That is, we have people who come into the church half-heartedly, just far enough in to get a kind of sprinkling of religion, but not far enough in to give their hearts and souls to Jesus Christ. They want the church to be there. They want the church to have good programs and good staff and nice facilities and plenty of parking, and they are glad for the church to help them in their time of need. But really, they want to keep God at arm's length, they don't want to get too close, they don't want to get too involved, they don't want to get too committed. They just want to come far enough in to get a little sprinkling of religion every now and then, and then, it's off to the cars and off to other interests.

This shallow approach to faith is not a new phenomenon. It's as old as the Bible itself. The rich young ruler knew that there was something missing in his life. He felt the emptiness and, bless his heart, knew that Jesus was the answer, but he couldn't bring himself to give his whole heart to Jesus, which is what is sorrowful about the rich young ruler's life.

How is it with you right now? Are you ready to give your heart completely to Jesus and follow him? Or are you trapped in a prison of your own making? Are you trapped in a prison of mixed-up priorities or pride or half-heartedness? If so, just remember this: Jesus came to set the prisoner free, and in that Christian freedom is found riches beyond counting!

6

Rich in Gratitude

Jesus and Zacchaeus

Scripture: Luke 19:1-10

I WANT TO BEGIN BY TELLING YOU ABOUT TWO OF MY MOST PRIZED possessions.

The first one is *a simple, ordinary rock.* It's a rock with some green and yellow paint splattered on it. I use it as a paperweight on my desk. I have had it for over thirty years. It's not worth a lot, but I cherish it. If I tried to sell it, I couldn't get much money for it, but you see, I would never even consider selling it, because I treasure it so much.

Why is it so special to me? Not because of what it is. Not because of how it looks. Not even because of what it does. But because of the one who gave it to me. That's what makes it special—the one who loved me and gave it to me.

Our son, Jeff, gave that green and yellow paperweight rock to me when he was five years old. He made it for me in Sunday school. It's the symbol of his love. The *giver,* not the gift, makes it special.

My second prized possession that I want to tell you about today is a *homemade greeting card.* I have also had it for over thirty years. I just love that card. I treasure that card so much because our daughter, Jodi, made it for me when she was six years old. On the front of the card, it reads, "To the Most Sweetest Father on Earth." And it has her own sketch of planet Earth. Inside, the words "Happy Birthday" are scratched through, and "Happy Father's Day" is written, followed by, "Oops! Everybody makes mistakes." And it is signed, "Love, Jodi (six years old)."

These gifts are special to me because of the special persons who gave them to me.

That is the real key to life, the real key to joy, the real key to genuine gratitude—to stress the giver rather than the gifts . . . for you see, we can gain the whole world and all the gifts but miss the giver and lose our own souls.

Celebrating the giver rather than the gift—that is the key. And when you make that breakthrough, you can never be the same. That kind of gratitude will change your life! There is a beautiful example of this in the Bible: the story of Zacchaeus in Luke 19. Remember the story with me.

Jesus and his disciples are heading toward the showdown in Jerusalem. As they pass through Jericho, they see that a great crowd has gathered to see Jesus. Zacchaeus is in the crowd. The scriptures tell us that Zacchaeus was a chief tax collector and was rich and that he was disliked and despised by his fellow townspeople. They resented paying taxes to Rome, and they felt that Zacchaeus, a fellow Jew, had betrayed them, had sold out to Rome, and had gotten rich at their expense. So they rejected him, shunned him, detested him. If you had conducted a popularity contest in Jericho that day, Zacchaeus may well have come in dead last.

This was the setting when Jesus came to Jericho that day. People had heard about Jesus and had gathered along the streets to see him. Zacchaeus was also eager to see the Nazarene, but Zacchaeus was short and couldn't see over the crowd. So Zacchaeus ran ahead and climbed into a sycamore tree in hopes of getting a glimpse of this great leader everyone was talking about.

When Jesus saw him, he sensed that Zacchaeus was the loneliest man in town, and his heart went out Zacchaeus. Jesus looked up and said, "Zacchaeus, make haste, and come down; for to day I must abide at thy house" (Luke 19:5 KJV). Zacchaeus was visibly touched, indeed, overwhelmed by this acceptance and this special honor. It had been a long time since anyone had been nice to him. Zacchaeus was so grateful, so filled with gratitude, that it changed his life.

Notice that Jesus gave him no material gifts. He gave him something better: love, respect, acceptance, and forgiveness. Zacchaeus became so grateful that his whole lifestyle changed. Why, it even touched his pocketbook. Before he had been a "taker," and he became a "giver."

That's the way it works. When we become truly grateful to God for the gift of his love, we can't be the same anymore! We are changed! We are turned around. We are converted, transformed. Zacchaeus was so grateful for Christ's acceptance of him and love for him that his life, his relationships, and his reason for living were all dramatically changed. That's what real gratitude does! It changes our lives! Let me show you what I mean.

First, Gratitude Gives Us a New Relationship with God

When you realize that God is loving, accepting, and forgiving, it changes your life. You don't have to be afraid or anxiety-ridden anymore. Gratitude becomes the lifeblood of your lifestyle. Zacchaeus learned it that day in Jericho, and it gave him a new relationship with God, a relationship not built on fear and appeasement, but built on love and grace.

Some years ago at St. Luke's, we started a new Sunday school class for special needs adults who need special education. Most of the class members live in an assisted-living center in Southwest Houston, and we send a van to pick them up and bring them to Sunday school and church every Sunday. They have made a treasured place for themselves in our St. Luke's family. They love to come here, and we love having them here. We named them the Joy Class, and they are well-named because they are a joy.

When we first started the class, there was a young man in the group named Sammy. Sammy came every Sunday, but he did not participate in the class at all. He seemed sad and suspicious, so he withdrew. He sat all by himself in the corner and stared at the floor. He would not sit at the table with the others. He would not eat the refreshments. He would not sing the songs. He would not speak to anybody or look at anybody. No matter how we tried, we could not connect with Sammy. We coaxed and reasoned and pleaded, but with no luck. Sammy would do absolutely nothing except sit in the corner all by himself and stare at the floor.

And then one day, everything changed, and it happened in the most unusual way. A volunteer in our church named Bill would go up to the Joy Class a few times each month to lead their song time. The class members really enjoyed singing, and Bill would play his banjo and sing songs with the class. They all loved it, except Sammy over in his corner. The class would sing songs such as "Jesus Loves Me," "Amazing Grace," "The Old Rugged Cross," "Sweet Hour of Prayer." All would sing along enthusiastically with Bill and his banjo, except Sammy.

Then one day, who knows why, Bill started playing his banjo and singing "Skip to My Lou." Bill had not planned to sing "Skip to My Lou" that morning. It just bubbled out of him And then the most amazing thing happened. Sammy jumped up out of his chair and did something no one in the class had ever seen him do before: he broke into a big smile! And then for the very first time, Sammy left his corner! He started skipping around the room, laughing and singing "Skip to My Lou" at the top of his voice. When the song was over, Sammy stopped skipping around the room, and he sat down at the table with the others! He joined the group! The class members and leaders were so excited, they all hugged him and welcomed him and patted him lovingly on the back. Sammy smiled broadly and from that point forward, he joyously and enthusiastically participated in everything the Joy Class did, right up until the time he moved away with his family to another city.

There was something about that song, "Skip to My Lou," that somehow touched something deep within Sammy and let him know that the Joy Class was a good thing for him. And from that point, he joined in and loved the class.

We were mystified and curious. We investigated and found that Sammy had loved his grandmother deeply and had lived with his grandmother right up until the time of her death. The day after her funeral, he was moved to the center in Southwest Texas. We also found out that when Sammy was a little boy, he would walk to Sunday school and church with his grandmother, and all the way there and back as they walked, he and his grandmother would sing "Skip to My Lou."

That song reminded him of the love and acceptance and joy he knew at church with his grandmother. When Bill and the class began singing that on that pivotal Sunday morning, Sammy suddenly realized that he was in Sunday school and church, and he then knew with confidence that this was a good place for him to be.

That experience gave Sammy a new relationship with the Joy Class and a new relationship with God. All of a sudden, the class became for Sammy a beautiful place and a beautiful group, the symbol of God's acceptance of him and God's love for him. The light bulb turned on, and Sammy realized, "This is church, and I'm loved here and valued here and treasured here!"

Something like that happened to Zacchaeus that day. As Jesus came to him and accepted him, that acceptance touched something deep within Zacchaeus and brought him back to his senses and back to God and caused him to see things differently.

Likewise, when we love God and accept his love for us, then we can suddenly see things differently. We see all the beautiful things he has graciously given us.

Everywhere we look, everything we see reminds us of God and all that he has lovingly prepared for us. Real gratitude gives us a new relationship with God and causes us to see miracles everywhere.

Albert Einstein once put it like this: "There are only two ways to live your life. One is as though nothing is a miracle. The other is as though everything is a miracle." That's the number one thing we learn from the Zacchaeus story. Real gratitude gives us a new relationship with God.

Second, Real Gratitude Gives Us a New Regard for Others

In the *Wizard of Id* comic strip, the priest asks, "Of all the major sins, which do you consider to be number one?"

"Well," came the reply, "They're all bad, but I think I like *greed* the best!"

Zacchaeus could have identified with that. He had been greedy. He had cheated. He had taken advantage of others. But then Jesus came to him and reached out to him and included him and ate with him—which in New Testament times was a dramatic symbol of forgiveness—and Zacchaeus was changed, redeemed, converted.

He was so grateful that Jesus had accepted him that he came down out of that sycamore tree with love in his heart. He had a new regard for others and said, "Behold, Lord, the half of my goods I give to the poor; and if I have defrauded any one of anything, I restore it four-fold" (v. 8 RSV). That's what real gratitude does for you. It enables you to see people differently. It causes you to see other people lovingly.

Some years ago, I ran across a story about a young college student who was visited by his father one weekend at a prestigious college in the east. The father had an old dilapidated car. When the dad drove away to go home, some of the boy's friends began to laugh and tease and make fun of that car. The young man said, "You can laugh if you want to, but let me tell you something. My father could have had a new car years ago if he had wanted one. He had the money to buy it, but he wanted me to have an education at this school more than he wanted a new car for himself. The only reason I am here is because he chose to drive that old car. I am so grateful to him because in that one generous sacrificial act, he taught me so much about life and thoughtfulness and love. I love that old car and I love the man in it."

That's just the way it works. The Zacchaeus story teaches us that real gratitude gives us a new relationship with God and a new regard for others.

Third and Finally, Real Gratitude Gives Us a New Reason for Living

Every now and then, I try to think of a new idea about what it means to be grateful. Here is my thought for this year: If gratitude is the *celebration* of God's generosity, then the Christian lifestyle is the *imitation* of God's generosity. That is, the best way to express our gratitude to God is to imitate, to model, to emulate his generosity in our daily living, to take on his gracious and generous approach, and to live daily in that spirit.

Zacchaeus got it! He saw it and did it! The question is, do we? Are we Godlike in our living?

Recently, I read a story about two men who were best friends. Bill and Tom had enjoyed each other's company since they were chil-dren. They had grown up together. They loved to hunt and fish. One Saturday morning, they went hunting, and there was an accident. As Bill was climbing over a barbed wire fence, he fell, and his gun went off. He shot himself in the leg and began to bleed profusely.

Tom rushed to Bill and made a tourniquet to slow the bleeding. Then, Tom picked Bill up, put Bill on his back, and carried him over two miles through rough terrain to get to their car, all the while saying, "You hang in there, Bill. Don't you die on me. I'm going to get you to the hospital, and we are going to get you well."

Tom tenderly got Bill in the car and rushed him to a nearby hospital for emergency surgery. It went well, and afterward the doctor told Bill that he would be all right and that he would recover nicely. The doctor also told Bill what Bill already knew, that Tom had saved his life!

Some years later, Tom had to undergo heart surgery. Bill stayed with Tom and Tom's wife around the clock for days and days. He would not leave the hospital. He would not leave his best friend. The medical staff at the hospital noticed this. They told Bill not to worry, that everything was going great for Tom. He was recovering beautifully. They told Bill that it was OK to leave and get some rest because he must be exhausted. Bill thanked them for their concern, and then he told them the story of how Tom had carried him on his back for over two miles to save his life years before. And then he said: "After what Tom did for me, there is nothing I would not do for him. If it weren't for Tom, I wouldn't be here today. I owe him everything. I owe him my life!"

That's how Zacchaeus felt about what Jesus did for him, and that is precisely how we as Christians gratefully feel because that is precisely what Jesus Christ has done for us. He has saved our lives, so there is nothing we would not do for him because he is the one who has given us a new relationship with God, a new regard for others, and a new reason for living. When you have those three things in your life, you are rich indeed in the things that count the most.

7
Rich in Generosity
The Widow's Gift

Scripture: Luke 21:1-4

Have you heard the story about the small girl, not more than ten or eleven years old, who was standing in a soup kitchen line in a poverty-stricken section of a large city? She was the last one in the long line. Many people had shown up that day, quite a few more than usual. The volunteers preparing and serving the food that day realized that the food was starting to run short. The servers were concerned.

The little girl did not seem to notice. Her attention was focused on three small children who were across the street, sitting and waiting for her in the shade under a big oak tree. The little girl continued to wait patiently in line that day, but when she finally made it to the servers, the only thing left was one banana. Without complaint, she took the single banana joyfully. With a smile and a nod, she thanked the volunteer servers, and then she walked back across the street to join the three smaller children.

Were they her siblings? Were they her friends? We don't know that, but what we do know is what the little girl did. Carefully, she peeled the banana. She broke it into three equal pieces, and she gave each of the other children one-third of the banana. Then, she sat down on the curb and licked the inside of the banana peel. A bystander who happened to witness that little girl's act of sacrificial love said later, "When I saw what that little girl did that day, I saw the face of God."

This touching story of the little girl who gave all of the banana away reminds me of the generous widow in Luke 21, who, in an act of trust and commitment and love, gave her all to God. Jesus saw what she did, and he was impressed by her strong faith.

Remember the story with me. Jesus and his disciples were at the temple one day. Our Lord was always looking for opportunities to teach his disciples the essence of our faith. On this particular day, Jesus and his disciples were watching people come to the offering box in the temple to place their gifts in the collection chests.

The noted historian Josephus described how in those days the temple had thirteen trumpet-shaped offering boxes to receive the gifts of the people. The worshipers who came with their gifts were from all different walks and stations of life. Some were educated, and some were not. Some were rich, and some were poor. But they all came. An important part of coming to the temple was to pass by the treasury and drop your money into the offering boxes.

Some put in large gifts, and bystanders could hear the rattling of the coins as they slid down and into the trumpet-shaped receptacles. The receptacles were rather narrow at the top and then got wider at the bottom. Some scholars believe they were shaped that way to prevent people from reaching in and taking money out. As people brought their offerings, you could tell by the sound of the coins hitting the bottom how large or how small each particular gift was.

Jesus and his disciples were positioned there (sitting off to the side) and watching the people parade by and make their gifts. Then, Jesus noticed her. He saw this poor widow approaching the treasury. He saw her drop in her two small coins—two pennies—and he was touched and impressed by what she had done. He leaned over and said to his disciples, "Truly I tell you, this poor widow has put in more than all of them" (Luke 21:3).

Jesus went on to explain that the rich people had given their gifts based on how much money they had left over once they had bought all of the food and entertainment and clothing and housing they needed and wanted; they gave out of the "leftovers." But this poor widow was more generous because she put God first and gave all she had.

Have you heard about the couple who called the Butterball turkey company hotline and said, "We have had a Butterball turkey in our freezer for twenty-three years. Is it safe to eat it?" The company representative said, "Has your freezer been on all the time?" "Oh, yes," the couple replied. "Well, then," said the representative, "it would be safe to eat it, but it probably wouldn't taste too good." "That's what we thought," the couple said, "So we'll just give it to the church."

That's what you call "leftover giving." And that kind of giving would not impress Jesus.

The generous widow, however, gave her first, her best, her all, to God. Her faith in God was so strong that she dared to give it all to God and then to trust God to be with her and help her. That kind of giving, that kind of generosity, that kind of faith, hope, and love touched the heart of Jesus and made this poor widow one of the heroes of the Bible.

In biblical times, the widows were often very poor. The patriarchal society back then would not encourage women to have a career, so many of them had no income. If husbands had died, they had no one to take care of them or provide for them. Some were young and had children to care for, and some were much older and were all alone. Their only way to survive was to rely on other people's charity. They needed other people to give them money, food, clothing, and other things so they could keep on living. In those days, for many of the widows, life was difficult and hard, and their faith in God was what kept them going.

Now, the question that jumps out of this famous Bible story of the widow's mite is: What was it about this woman and her gift that so touched the heart of Jesus? What was it about her gift that day that prompted Jesus to encourage his disciples to learn from her faith and to be like her? Let me pinpoint three ideas.

First of All, Her Generous Gift Was a Reflection of Her Trust

According to the story, a plane was flying from San Francisco to Los Angeles. There had been a forty-five-minute delay and everybody on board was frustrated. Unexpectedly, the plane then had to make an unscheduled stop in Sacramento on the way. The flight attendant explained that there would be another forty-five-minute delay and if the passengers wanted to get off the plane, they could deplane, stretch their legs, move around a bit, and then reboard in thirty minutes.

Everybody got off the plane except one gentleman who was blind. You could tell that this man had flown this flight many times before because the pilot approached him, called him by name, and said, "Keith, we're going to be here in Sacramento for almost an hour. Would you like to get off and stretch your legs?" Keith replied, "No thanks, but maybe my dog would like to walk out and move around a bit?" The pilot said, "Well, I'll be glad to walk him for you."

Now picture this: All the passengers are out there waiting around in the gate area when suddenly they look up to see the pilot of their flight walk off the plane with a seeing-eye dog while he is wearing sunglasses! Immediately, the people stared and then they gulped and then they scattered. In a panic, they rushed off through the terminal not only to change planes, but also to change airlines!

Now, the people obviously misread the situation and overreacted. There was no real danger, no real problem, but what they saw that day shook them up, and they lost their sense of trust in that airline.

This can happen in the church. People can lose their trust because they misread something; and they scatter, they desert, they drop out, they run away. Their trust is shaken, and they rush off to try something else.

Some years ago, I saw a movie. I don't remember the name of the movie. It was a comedy and had a comic scene that was repeated over and over throughout the film—naive, gullible older woman watching TV. And she was doing whatever was being advertised on TV. In one scene, she had bright green hair as she watched a hair dye commercial. Another scene showed her shaving her face, trying out the new shaving cream being promoted in the TV ad. One other scene depicted her brushing her teeth with purple foam toothpaste as she watched the commercial promoting that.

Everybody in the theater laughed each time because the scenes were humorous in that movie. Sadly, that same kind of thing happens to some people in their spiritual lives. They gullibly, naively chase after one new religious fad after another, failing to trust the tried and true faith, failing to trust the way, the truth, and the life.

In this generous widow, we see her deep trust in God. Obviously, life had not been a bed of roses for her. She had known hardship and grief and poverty, and yet she kept on keeping the faith. She kept on believing and serving and giving. She kept on trusting God.

Some years ago, I heard a story about a granddad who went for a walk one morning with his four-year-old granddaughter. As grandfathers will do with their granddaughters, he decided to teach her something helpful. They had walked several blocks away from home. Suddenly, granddad said to her, "Julie, do you know where you are?

"No, sir," answered little Julie.

Then grandfather asked a second question: "Julie, do you know how to get home from here?"

Again Julie answered, "No, sir."

"Well," said granddad, "if you don't know where you are and you don't know how to get home from here, then that can only mean one thing. You must be lost."

"No, Granddad," answered Julie, "I can't be lost, because I'm with you!"

Isn't that beautiful? I love that story because it's about childlike trust. The Christian faith tells us that we can trust God like that. It tells us that if we stay close to God (come what may), we can't be lost. That's the first thing that's so impressive and touchng about this widow and her gift. Her gift was a reflection of her trust.

Second, Her Gift Was a Reflection of Her Commitment

Her commitment was unwavering, unflinching, unconditional. It was not a "fair weather" commitment that she expressed only when all the breaks and blessings were coming her way. Her commitment was solid, sturdy, strong, unshakeable. Even though times were tough, she was committed to her God, her church, her faith.

A friend of mine tells about an experience he had at a local shopping mall. While his wife was shopping, he sat down on one of those benches in the middle of the mall to "people watch." He was seated next to a booth that sells sunglasses. A young couple walked up to the booth to check out the sunglasses. The young man had spiked hair, standing straight up in all directions. His hair was green and orange and red and pink and purple. He had rings in his ears, his nose, his lips, and his eyebrows, and he had tattoos on both arms.

51

The young man tried on a pair of sunglasses and turned to let his girlfriend see how they looked on him. She said, "Oh, honey, take those off quick! They make you look weird!"

My friend said that in that moment, the phrase "Beauty is in the eye of the beholder" suddenly took on a whole new meaning.

When that widow put in her two coins that day, some people probably looked at her and said, "Isn't that pitiful? Isn't that weird? What a sorry gift that was! If I couldn't do any better than that, I'd just stay home." But not Jesus. He saw great beauty in her gift. He saw something quite exquisite in her gift. He saw great faith in her gift. He saw an important lesson for his disciples then and now to learn—the beauty and power of deep commitment.

In the 1984 Los Angeles Olympic games, a woman marathon runner named Gabriela Anderson staggered into the stadium long after the other runners had either finished the race or quit. She was so exhausted that it took her six minutes to finish the last four hundred meters. People shouted for her to quit the race, to sit down and rest because somebody else had won the race long ago. But Gabriela Anderson refused to quit. She was determined to finish her race. And that day she gave us all a lesson in courage and perseverance and commitment.

It's so easy to quit and throw in the towel when life is hard. There are people right now who are ready and tempted to quit their jobs, their marriages, their schools, their friendships, their churches, their faith because sometimes life is tough. But the lesson that the generous widow and Gabriela Anderson give us, the lesson Jesus saw and pointed out to his disciples, was simply this: "Don't quit! Don't give out! Don't give in! Just keep on putting one foot in front of the other. Come what may in this life, hang in there." Don't give up on your trust, and don't give up on your commitment! The generous widow's gift that day reflected her trust and her commitment.

Third and Finally, Her Generous Gift Was a Reflection of Her Love

The widow loved God and loved the temple, and because of that love, she wanted to do her part. Jesus saw her spirit of love that day, and he was touched and moved and impressed.

His name is Charles. Charles is a member of our church. He is a mentor in our Kids Hope USA program. Every week, he goes to a nearby elementary school to be a friend, an encourager, and a mentor to a little boy named Roberto. Roberto is ten years old. Charles and Roberto have bonded in a beautiful way. Though there is quite a difference in their ages, Charles has become Roberto's best friend.

In addition to having Charles as his mentor, Roberto also has a prayer partner provided by our church. Roberto's prayer partner happens to be my wife, June. June prays for Roberto and Charles every day, and sometimes she sends little gifts to Roberto. Roberto has not received a lot of gifts in his life, so he is always thrilled when one comes.

Early this year, they had a party in Roberto's class at school. The room mother brought punch and cookies, and she brought some colorful decorated paper party napkins. Roberto had never before seen a beautiful napkin like that, and he loved it, and it became his prized possession! He kept it with him at all times. For days and days and days, Roberto carried that paper party napkin in his pocket. He probably kept it under his pillow at night. He loved that napkin and was so proud of it!

And then, a few weeks ago, Charles told Roberto that his prayer partner, June, was in the hospital, having undergone major surgery. Roberto, with Charles's help, created a homemade get-well card for June out of a piece of construction paper. When June opened the card, guess what she found in it. That's right, that party napkin! In the spirit of love and concern, ten-year-old Roberto gave June his prized possession. In the spirit of love, like the generous widow in the New Testament, Roberto gave all he had!

Let me ask you something. Do you know how to love like that? That's what impressed Jesus that day when he saw the widow make her gift. In that act of giving, he saw her trust, her commitment, and her love; and he wanted all of his disciples to be like that. He wanted them rich in these things that money can't buy.

8
Rich in Friendship
The Rooftop Friends

Scripture: Mark 2:1-12

I ONCE HEARD A STORY ABOUT A WOMAN IN RURAL FLORIDA WHO WAS AT home recuperating from a lengthy illness. She was sitting in her wheelchair on the front porch of the family home watching her son work on his automobile.

The car was up on blocks, and he was lying underneath. For some reason, the car suddenly lurched forward and fell on top of her son's body, threatening to crush the life out of him. The woman screamed for help, and her husband came running. He tried to lift the car but could not. So, in a panic, he drove off to find help.

Hearing her son's cry for help, the woman (who was quite frail from her long siege of poor health) nevertheless raised herself up out of her wheelchair and stood to her feet. It was the first time she had stood without assistance in many weeks. She walked unsteadily to the car. Bracing herself, she lifted that car just a few inches, but enough for her son to scramble free. Then she collapsed and fell to the ground. Moments later, she was rushed to the hospital. After a thorough examination, she was released with only some strained muscles. The doctor said, "I will always wonder how high she might have lifted that car had she been well and strong!"

Now, this story reminds us dramatically of the power of love. It shows us graphically what we can do and what we will do when we are properly motivated by love. That's what this story of the "rooftop friends" in Mark 2 is really all about. Motivated by their love for their friend who was paralyzed, the four friends took a risk; they went out

55

on a limb for their buddy. Because of their boldness, their courage, their persistence, and because of their faith, their friendship, their love, a miracle took place!

Remember the story with me. It was one of those remarkable events in the ministry of Jesus that was so vivid, so dramatic, and so unforgettable that three of the Gospel writers include it in their narratives.

In the first chapter of Mark, Jesus begins his ministry. He goes through Galilee preaching, teaching, and healing. Word spreads like wildfire about his eloquent words and his power to heal. People come seeking him out.

Jesus comes to Capernaum and while at home there, a large group of people come to see him and to hear him. They are jammed shoulder to shoulder in the house, at the doors, and looking in the windows—a huge throng of people, a solid mass of humanity. They are all there, listening to Jesus speak, when suddenly, they hear a noise above them and look up. Imagine their amazement when they see the roof being opened up and a man who is paralyzed being lowered on his pallet down into the presence of Jesus.

Four of his friends have brought him to Jesus. They couldn't get in the regular way, so they lower him down to the Master through the roof. The people in the large crowd are astonished, some are probably aggravated by the disruption, but Jesus shows no surprise or unhappiness. Jesus likes it! He is touched by the love, the ingenuity, the stubborn faith, the can-do spirit of these four friends who will not be denied. They so love their friend who is paralyzed, and they so believe in Jesus' power to help him, and they so recognize the specialness of this moment and this opportunity that they will not quit. Ingeniously, heroically, they find a way to get it done.

Jesus' heart goes out to all of them, and he says to the man on the pallet: "My son, your sins are forgiven. Stand up, take up your mat and walk" (paraphrase of Mark 2:6, 9, 11). And he does!

End of story. And they all lived happily ever after? No, not quite. The scribes and Pharisees are upset with Jesus. They murmur in the background, talk behind his back, and plot against him. So that's not quite the end. Many things could be noted and examined here. For example

⑤ We could look at the relationship between forgiveness and healing. Was there something in this man's life causing him to be immobilized? Why did Jesus say, "My son, your sins are forgiven," as he healed the man?

⑤ Or, we could look at Jesus' creative way of handling interruptions. He was so good at that. Some of the greatest things Jesus did and taught occurred as he dealt productively and redemptively with interruptions.

⑤ Or, we could look at the conflict between Jesus and the religious authorities of the day. The watchdogs of orthodox religion became so hostile toward Jesus. Why?

All of these are important, but for now, let's zero in on the portrait of heroic Christian love painted beautifully and boldly for us by the creative action of these four friends.

First of All, They Were "Tuned In"

These four friends were tuned in to the specialness of this moment, tuned in to the uniqueness of this opportunity, tuned in to the need of their friend.

Many years ago, as the story goes, a young Morse code operator named John heard that a shipping company was advertising a job opening. He was interested. However, when John arrived at the main office to apply, he found a large number of applicants ahead of him in a crowded waiting room. There was a sign on a desk that instructed the applicants to sign in and be seated and wait till they were summoned for an interview.

John signed in and took a seat on a bench next to the counter, and then as he waited, he gradually became aware of the faint tapping of a telegraph machine on the desk. After a few minutes of concentration, John suddenly stood up and stepped through the office door behind the counter. One of the other applicants noticed what John had done and pointed it out to the others. They wondered, *What on earth was this man doing marching into the office like that without being called? Who did he think he was? They will probably throw him out on his ear immediately.*

57

A few minutes later, the door opened, and two men—the owner of the shipping company and John—stepped into the waiting room. The owner raised his hand to get the attention of the crowd. "Thank you for coming in today, gentlemen," he said in a loud voice, "but the position has been filled by this young man named John."

"Wait a minute," the applicants all protested at once. "We don't get it. This is not right. We were all here before John even came in, and we never got a chance to talk to anyone. It's not fair!"

The owner said, "Oh, it was indeed fair. On our ships, a Morse code operator has to be alert constantly while on duty, and this young man has proved that he is. You see, for the past hour, ever since we opened the doors to you, we've been sending a Morse code message over the telegraph here. It said, 'If you understand this message, then come right in. The job is yours.' John here is obviously the only one who was alert enough to hear the message above the noise of the crowd. So he gets the job!"

John was "tuned in." So were the rooftop friends. They were tuned in to the need of their friend, so tuned in that they didn't wait to be asked. They saw the need, the opportunity to help, and they responded. They realized that this was it, this was their big chance to help their friend, and they grabbed it, they seized the moment.

On top of that, look at how "tuned in" Jesus was. The traditional story about this passage was that the paralytic was a stonemason. He was a devout man but was forced by Herod to work on the Sabbath. This bothered him. He felt guilty about working on the Lord's Day, but he was afraid to disobey Herod and the power of Rome. According to this traditional story, the man was injured on the Sabbath, and then he felt even more guilt. He felt that God was angry with him and that God was punishing him for breaking the fourth commandment. So his paralysis was not only physical, but also spiritual. Whatever his physical ailment may have been, he was also immobilized by his guilt and remorse and fear and shame. And that's why when Jesus healed him, he said, "My son, your sins are forgiven."

Jesus met his need, met him where he was, and gave him what he most needed because, in essence, Jesus was saying to him, "It's OK. God is not angry with you. God loves you. God forgives you. You can have new life. The Father is not against you. He is all for you. You are forgiven. You are made whole. So, rise, get up, take up your pallet, and walk."

That's the first thing we notice here—a key ingredient of love and friendship. Number one is to be tuned in, to be sensitive to the needs of others.

Second, the Rooftop Friends Were Persistent

The four friends refused to give up when they saw that big crowd surrounding the house. They would not quit. They would not be denied. They were totally committed to their friend and to their task. They loved their friend so much that they were determined to find a way, and they did find a way! Their persistence paid off. It usually does.

Are you familiar with the name Tony Allen? He was a basketball player at Oklahoma State University and an exceptional athlete. He was named Player of the Year in the Big 12 Conference his senior year, an honor awarded by a vote of the coaches. Many would say he was the primary reason Oklahoma State had such a great year in basketball in 2004. But the Tony Allen you see today is quite different—amazingly different—from the Tony Allen of ten years ago.

Tony was a troublemaker. He grew up in a rough neighborhood in which he was exposed to one bad influence after another. Many of his childhood friends are in prison now. Before going to Oklahoma State, Tony got into trouble and was kicked off the Butler Community College basketball team. He transferred to Wabash College, where his trouble continued.

In a way, it's amazing that Oklahoma State recruited him and especially amazing that he was allowed to stay on the team because just days before his first class at OSU, he was arrested for his role in a parking lot riot at a restaurant that involved three hundred people. Tony Allen was arrested for obstruction, assault, and resisting an officer. The college decided to give him one more chance, and thank God they did, because Tony Allen's life was turned completely around.

When the Oklahoma State seniors were honored before the Texas A&M game on March 6, Tony Allen came onto the court with his mother, Ella, and his sisters, Ebony and Dominique. His mother said, "The Tony I see today is not the Tony I knew ten years ago, thanks to God. By the grace of God it's worked out better than I could have ever thought in a million years. Tony had a lot of kinks to work out. Thanks to God the change has been tremendous. It makes me want to cry" ("Saving Faith," *Thrust*, March 24, 2004, pp. 3, 6).

How did it occur? What caused this amazing turnaround of Tony Allen's life? Well, interestingly it happened because of a persistent friend. The equipment manager for the Oklahoma State basketball team kept asking Tony Allen to go to church with him. Time and again, Tony Allen declined. But that young equipment manager would not give up. He kept on asking. He kept on inviting, and finally one day, Tony Allen went to church with his persistent friend.

There he heard the stories of Jesus, and he was captivated. He went back to church and then back again, and then in September of 2004, Tony Allen accepted Jesus Christ as his Lord and Savior. He was baptized and joined the church, and he became a committed Christian. "It had me in tears," he said. "After all the bad things I had done, I felt it was time to get baptized. My body just felt clean. I felt like a new person."

Tony Allen became a new person indeed, a role model for kids, a humble person who now tries to be loving and caring and respectful to everyone he meets. That persistent friend made all the difference by getting Tony Allen into the presence of Christ. And that is precisely what those rooftop friends did long ago because they were "tuned in" and were persistent.

Third and Finally, They Were Servants

They were not prima donnas; they were servants. Every time we hire somebody to come on our staff at St. Luke's, we hire that person in my office so I can give my "servant theology speech." I say that we want everyone to wear two hats at the same time: first, the kingdom of God hat, which means you do whatever is needed to help the kingdom of God; second, the hat of the particular job we are asking that person to do at this time (youth ministry, children's ministry, music, evangelism, education, or whatever).

Then, I will say, "Let me illustrate that. If I'm walking down the hallway on the way to the church service on Sunday morning, and if I see that someone has placed a half-full cup of coffee on the carpet, what do I do? Do I put on my prima donna hat and say, 'I didn't go to seminary to pick up after other people?' No! I never do that, because I believe in servant theology. So instead, I put on my kingdom of God hat and pick it up before somebody kicks it over because that helps the kingdom of God."

And sometimes on Sunday mornings, I walk to church. And sometimes when I walk across the front lawn at 6:30 or 7:00 in the morning, I will discover a whiskey bottle and a couple of empty beer cans in the front yard of our church. I don't know why people do that. I guess the state they are in on Saturday night makes them think that it's funny to throw whiskey bottles and beer cans in the church's front yard on a Saturday night. Well, I put on my kingdom of God hat and pick up the trash, so the front of the church will look beautiful (as it should) when people arrive later to come to Sunday school and church. Now, it is interesting to see the expression on people's faces when they see me walking into the church on Sunday morning with an empty whiskey bottle and two empty beer cans in my hands. And then I have to decide whose trash can to put them in!

But, you see, the point is clear. As Christians, we are called to be servants, servants of Christ, servants of his church, servants of God's kingdom.

We are not "above" doing anything that helps the cause of Christ. We do whatever it takes to help God's kingdom. If it means mopping a floor, picking up trash, arranging chairs, helping someone find a meeting room, holding an umbrella for somebody, or carrying a friend into the presence of Jesus Christ, then that's what we do because we as Christians are called first and foremost to be servants!

If all Christians everywhere understood that and embraced that "servant theology concept," we could change the world!

Well, how is it with you? Are you tuned in to God's special moment? Are you persistent and determined? Are you willing to be a servant? I hope so because there is an incredible richness of spirit in that kind of friendship. It is wealth beyond counting.

9

Rich in Real Life

I Hope You Live All of Your Life

Scripture: Luke 10:25-28

Some years ago, Art Linkletter wrote a book that became an instant best seller. It was entitled *Kids Say the Darndest Things!* (Berkeley, Calif.: Celestial Arts, 2005). He was right. They do! And sometimes they are able to put into words what others are thinking but are afraid to say.

For example, there is a story about a young mother in Arkansas who recently overheard her two daughters talking about marriage. The two girls were four and six. The six-year-old rather philosophically asked, "Which would you rather have, a rich husband or good eyes?" Then she answered her own question by stating, "I would choose good eyes." But her four-year-old sister said dryly, "I'll take a rich husband and contact lenses!"

Then there was that little eight-year-old girl named Patty who was noted in her community for her blunt, surprising, and disarming comments. They made a whole list of "Patty sayings." Perhaps the best was something she said at church one morning. They had a guest preacher that Sunday who had two agonizingly obvious characteristics: he preached loud, and he preached long. On this particular Sunday morning, the guest preacher was droning on and on and on, loud and long. He was preaching the sermon "If I Sat Where You Sit." Every few minutes he would dramatically repeat that phrase, "If I sat where you sit," over and over he said it. After about forty-five minutes of that, eight-year-old Patty had had enough; she turned and said to her mother in a stage whisper, "If he says that one more time, he can sit where I'm sitting because I'm going home!" And I expect Patty would have taken some folks with her about that time.

But the saying of a child that I really want to call to your attention is one that was quoted some years ago by Dr. Halford Luccock. He once told the story about a little girl who wrote a letter to her favorite uncle. At the close of the letter she said, "I love you very, very much, and I hope you live all of your life!"

That was a wonderful wish, wasn't it? "I hope you live all of your life." Actually, if we go back to the New Testament, we discover that Jesus Christ came to earth to make that wish come true for us.

The scriptures tell us over and over again that real life, abundant life, eternal life, meaningful life—whatever we may call it—is found in Jesus Christ. And in our scripture lesson in Luke 10:27, Jesus gives us a clear-cut formula for zestful and purposeful living. He shows us here that the way to life is to love God with all our heart, soul, mind, and strength, and to love our neighbors as we love ourselves. And then he adds, "Do this and you will live." Do this and you will live all your life.

Now, the question that explodes out of this text for you and me this morning is simply this: Are we dead or alive spiritually? How do we come alive spiritually? How do we find the abundant life Jesus came to bring us? How do we do more than just exist, endure, cope, or get by? How do we really live all of our lives?

Let me break this down a bit and bring it closer to home for us because implicit in this text is a great summary of the Christian lifestyle.

First of All, to Have Real Life, We Need a Healthy Love for Self

We need to have a healthy self-esteem, to get a right sense of our own importance. Christ came to show us that we are valuable to God. He went to the cross to show us how much he values us.

It's a great day in a person's life when he or she realizes that you don't have to dress fancy, you don't have to put on airs, you don't have to drive a fancy car or live in an elegant home or be invited to all the parties in order to have a real sense of value. It's a great day in a person's life when just being made by God is enough.

A minister friend of mine went to visit the Smithsonian Institute in Washington, D.C. a few years ago. He was fascinated with the museum of history and technology and their outstanding displays of historical objects and inventions. The gowns of the Presidents' wives, the early telephones of Alexander Graham Bell, the amazing inventions of Thomas Edison, and the writings of Benjamin Franklin all impressed him greatly.

But, he said the one thing that caught his attention and interested him most was a little wooden whistle in a big glass case, a little wooden whistle lying there on a piece of velvet. At first, he couldn't figure out why it was there. What was so special about a small simple wooden whistle? But then an attendant turned on the light, and he could read the small print on the little card under the whistle. It said, "Handmade by George Washington." Then he understood. Then it took on value. Then he could appreciate why it was there on display in the Smithsonian Institute: George Washington had made it by hand.

Well, you and I are handmade by God! Jesus came to show us that we are God's handiwork, and that's what makes us special.

Unfortunately, there are some people who never understand that, and consequently they have such an unhealthy opinion of themselves that they are on edge all the time, angry all the time, and are constantly getting their feelings hurt and always feeling slighted

Their low self-esteem makes them miserable, and they take it out on everybody they meet. More and more, psychologists are telling us that we can't feel good about life until we feel good about ourselves.

Remember in the Gospels how Jesus said, "If you go to a dinner, take the lowest seat." He didn't mean to do that because you have a low opinion of yourself. No. He meant do that because you have such a healthy opinion of yourself that it doesn't really matter where you sit. It doesn't really matter if folks don't recognize you or cater to you. When you get to that point, pettiness goes away and then you can really live.

You see, the point is clear. Jesus was teaching us that we don't have to have recognition or position or accolades, because we know that we are handmade by God, and because of that we can feel good about ourselves. We can be at home with ourselves and at peace with ourselves. We can have a healthy love for self.

That's number one: an important ingredient in living all your life is a healthy love for self.

Second, to Have Real Life We Need a Healthy Love for Others

Dr. Michael Brown, a minister friend of mine in North Carolina, tells about a touching moment he had shortly after his father had died. Michael was in deep grief. He had loved his dad dearly, and now suddenly his father was gone. A family in his church urged him to use their beach house to get away and to rest, relax, reflect, and regroup. He took them up on their offer and went alone to their beautiful "home away from home."

One day while there, he went into town for lunch. Racked with the pain of a broken heart, he was standing alone in a buffet line. His head hung down low, and he was ready to cry again. He was missing his dad so much and wishing his father were standing there with him in the buffet line.

Suddenly there was a voice like an angel's, and maybe it was an angel's voice. "Hi, my name is Alicia. I'm three years old. What's your name?" Michael looked down into the big brown eyes of this beautiful little girl with her hair in braids. She was smiling up at him. She walked over without being asked, hugged Michael's leg, and then extended her arms for Michael to pick her up. Her mom nodded that it was OK, so Michael reached down and picked her up.

Three-year-old Alicia softly nestled her head on Michael's shoulder. He just stood there and hugged her, remembering what it was like to hold his boys that way, and remembering what it was like when his father's strong arms held him that way when he was a little boy. Michael stood there, holding Alicia. Her mom was apologetic. She said to Michael, "I'm sorry. Sometimes Alicia is too friendly." And then she said, "Alicia, come on now. You need to get down."

Michael looked at Alicia's mom and mouthed the words so Alicia could not hear but her mom could: "My father died last week. I needed this hug." So her mom just stood there and smiled as her three-year-old daughter surprised a grieving stranger with the gift of love, with a hug he desperately needed in that place and at that moment. Later Michael said, "I believe God was hugging me through Alicia."

That's our calling as Christians: to be the instruments of God's love, of God's encouragement, of God's compassion, and of God's healing and to be the instruments of God's hug. The hymn writer C. D. Meigs put it like this: "Help me to live for others (Lord) / That I may live like Thee."

To live—to really live—we need a healthy love for self and a healthy love for others.

Third and Finally, to Have Real Life, We Need a Healthy Love for God

Dr. Fred Craddock once told about a little boy who at long last reached the age of eight. Finally, eight years old! He was finally able to play Little League baseball. He already had a cap, but it was much too large for his head. If it weren't for his ears, he would have smothered. He also had a glove. He stood in front of the mirror, and he popped his fist into his glove. He waited and waited that eternity before baseball practice began.

He worried his mother to death.

"When are we going to practice?"

"Practice is next Tuesday, Jimmy, next Tuesday afternoon."

"I'd better call the coach."

"Hey, Coach, this is Jimmy. When are we going to practice?"

"Next Tuesday afternoon at 5:00, Jimmy."

"Thanks, Coach. You can count on me. I'll be there."

Jimmy was so excited to get to play baseball, he slept in his baseball cap and wore his glove constantly. And every day he asked his mother when baseball practice was. And then he called the coach to ask him. He was wearing everybody into the ground, but each time they told him, "Five o'clock next Tuesday afternoon, Jimmy."

Finally, Tuesday afternoon arrived, and it began to sprinkle. At 3:30, it really began to rain hard. By 4:30, it was a downpour. Jimmy's mother was ironing. She said, "Jimmy, I really am sorry that it's raining so hard. I know how disappointed you must be. Jimmy? Jimmy?"

He was already out the door, his cap on his head, his glove on the handlebars of his bicycle. Off in the rain he went. The practice field was on the school grounds. The coach lived across the street. The coach looked out the window that afternoon and decided it was raining much too hard to practice. But as the coach watched the rain pelting down, he saw something. He saw a small boy standing all alone where home plate once was. The boy was up to his knees in mud and water.

The coach said to his wife, "Some crazy kid is over there on the ball field. I guess I'd better go rescue him." The coach put on his boots and raincoat, grabbed his umbrella, and swam over to Jimmy. "Jimmy, what are you doing here? Can't you see it's too wet? It's pouring. We can't practice in this weather!" Jimmy looked up at his coach and said, "I told you I'd be here, Coach. I told you that you could count on me. I promised. I gave you my word!"

Let me tell you something. I don't know where Jimmy is today, but I hope he hasn't changed. I hope Jimmy hasn't learned how to water down his commitments or make excuses. The simple straightforward response of that little boy to his coach was: "I told you I would be here. I told you that you could count on me. I gave you my word. I promised."

That's the kind of allegiance, the kind of commitment, the kind of devotion, and the kind of love we as Christians are called upon to have for God. Jesus put it like this: "You shall love the Lord your God with all your heart, and with all your soul, and with all your strength, and with all your mind" (Luke 10:27).

All of us who have been members of the church at one time in our lives stood at the altar and made a fourfold promise to God. We stood at God's altar and promised to be loyal to him and to support him and his church with our prayers, our presence, our gifts, and our service. No mistake about it. We promised that. We said to God, "I will be here. You can count on me. I give you my word."

Let me ask you something. What would happen if we all took that promise seriously? If we were totally committed to God and his church like Jimmy was committed to his coach and his Little League baseball team, we could turn the world upside down! If we put God first and loved God that completely, that would really be something, and we would really, really come alive because that's what it means to have real life in Christ. It means to have a healthy love for self, a healthy love for others, and a healthy love for God.

10

Rich in "Because Of" Faith

Do You Have an "In Order To" Faith
or a "Because Of" Faith?

Scripture: 1 Thessalonians 5:16-18

SOME YEARS AGO, I WAS ASKED TO SPEAK TO A GROUP OF GRADUATING high school seniors. I wanted to share with them and with all in the audience one of the greatest spiritual insights, one of the most powerful theological breakthroughs, one of the most moving "light bulb moments" of my life. I will never forget it. It happened years ago when I was in seminary. It happened in a class called Systematic Theology.

My theology professor was a wonderful man. Whoever came up with the phrase "Christian Gentleman" must have had someone like him in mind. He was a deeply spiritual man, a most humble man, who started and ended every class with the most beautiful and heartwarming prayers, and who treated every student with grace, dignity, compassion, and kindness. Everybody on campus loved and respected this brilliant and modest professor of theology. He had a sharp mind when it came to Christian doctrines and beliefs, but he was not the least bit interested in fashion.

He had only two suits; one was black and the other was royal blue. Somehow over the years (because he was color-blind), he got the coats and pants mixed up. So, one day he would wear the black coat and the royal blue pants, and the next day he would wear the blue coat and the black pants, prompting the students privately and affectionately to refer to him as "Dr. Bruise" because he was always black and blue.

I learned many things "sitting at his feet" in the lecture hall and in the seminary coffee shop and in his office. But nothing has stayed with me more vividly than what he did one particular morning. It changed my life and my whole approach to the Christian faith, and I want to pass that on to you.

He came into the classroom that morning decked out in black and blue, and he led the class in a beautiful prayer. Then he went to the chalkboard and drew a large cross in the center of the board. Under the cross, he wrote "God's Love." Next, he moved way over to the extreme left side of the chalkboard and drew a series of arrows moving toward the cross. Above the arrows he wrote "Good Works," and underneath the arrows, he wrote these three words: "In Order To."

The professor then proceeded to make a series of arrows moving away from the cross toward the right side of the chalkboard. Above the arrows on the right side, he wrote "Good Works," and under this set of arrows, he wrote two words: "Because Of." The professor stepped back from the chalkboard and stared intently for several moments at what he had created. There was a deep, consecrated silence in the room as all of us young theology students surveyed what our beloved professor had drawn and tried to figure out what on earth it all meant.

Slowly, the professor turned toward us and said, "Ladies and gentlemen, do you have an 'in order to' faith or a 'because of' faith?" How would you answer that question? Well, there was total silence in the classroom that day because none of us students back then had the foggiest notion or the faintest idea of what he was talking about.

The professor realized that quickly, and he said, "Let me help you. The cross represents God's Love. The arrows stand for Good Works. So the question is, Do you do good works in order to win God's love? Or do you do good works because you already have God's love?" The professor paused for a moment, and then he said, "Ladies and gentlemen, I'm trying to move you from an 'in order to' faith to a 'because of' faith. You see," he said, "we love God 'because' he first loved us. We don't do good works to try to win God's love.

We do good works because we already have God's love and because we are so grateful to God for his amazing grace, so grateful to God for what he has already done for us in Jesus Christ that we can't sit still. We can't wait to serve him and share him with others."

In a nutshell, he said this is what Christianity really is. It is responsive gratitude. We are so grateful to God for what he has done for us in Jesus Christ that we can't wait to serve him and share him with others.

When I was a teenager, I loved my parents because they were my parents, because they first loved me, because I was so grateful to them for all they had done for me, given to me, and sacrificed for me. That's why I loved them, not in order to get the car Friday night.

A great biblical example of this is Bartimaeus. Remember him? He was blind and a beggar, until Jesus came and healed him. Then notice how that story ends. Bartimaeus was so grateful to Jesus for what Jesus had done for him that he became a disciple. He couldn't sit still. He dropped everything and followed Jesus. Now, why did he do that? Not in order to win Jesus' love. He already had that. He followed Jesus because of gratitude. Once he was blind and now because of Jesus, he could see.

That's why we follow and serve Jesus today—because of gratitude! When you understand that grateful living concept, when you take on that *because of* mind-set, when you commit your heart and soul to that, it will change your life and will change your approach to everything.

What greater illustration of this could there be than the apostle Paul? Paul was hunting down Christians and executing them. He was a self-proclaimed vigilante trying to stamp out the Christian movement. But then the risen Lord appeared to Paul on the Damascus Road and said in effect, "Paul, I know all about you. I know what you've been doing. I know how you have been working against me. But still, I love you, I need you, and I want you on my side."

Paul was bowled over by that love, that grace, that forgiveness, and that acceptance. When he came face to face with Jesus Christ, the One he had been persecuting, Paul expected the axe to fall. Only it wasn't an axe that fell. It was a gracious invitation. "Come on, Paul, and join us. Be one of us." Paul never forgot the sheer incredible joy and astonishment of that moment. He spent the rest of his life trying in gratitude to bowl over the world as he had been bowled over that day by God's amazing grace. Later, he wrote a letter to the Thessalonians, and in that letter he gave them and us a great formula for living that sums it all up, a great three-point philosophy of life that those graduates I was speaking to, and all of us, would do well to live by every day. Here's what he said: Because we are so grateful to God, we can rejoice always, pray without ceasing, and give thanks in all circumstances.

Let's take a look at each of these.

First, Rejoice Always

The great writer Teilhard de Chardin put it like this: "Joy is the most infallible sign of the presence of God."

At the Super Bowl Prayer Breakfast in Houston last January, someone told a funny story about Bart Starr, the great NFL quarterback who led the Green Bay Packers to five NFL titles and two Super Bowl victories. He was Most Valuable Player in the first two Super Bowls. When Bart Starr quarterbacked the Packers to their second Super Bowl championship, a close friend of his was away on business in China. He wanted to write a letter to congratulate Bart Starr, but he didn't have the Starrs' Green Bay mailing address with him in China. So he simply addressed the letter to "The Greatest Quarterback in the World." He didn't put Green Bay or Wisconsin or USA on the envelope, just those words, "The Greatest Quarterback in the World." And can you believe it, the letter arrived in Bart Starr's mailbox a few days later. When Bart Starr arrived home that afternoon, his wife ran out waving that letter, all excited, and she said, "Bart, you are not going to believe this. We just got a letter for Johnny Unitas!"

Now, how do we know that story? The only way we could. Bart Starr and his wife told that story themselves and got a good laugh out of it because as Christians and devoted church people, they have learned how to "rejoice always." Each year on the Saturday before the Super Bowl, the Athletes in Action organization presents an award to the NFL player who exemplifies service to God, church, family, and community. It's called the Bart Starr Award.

Another great example of what it means to "rejoice always" is found in a man named Robert, who is a missionary. When he speaks, he begins with this sentence: "I have everything I need for joy!" This is amazing because this man lives out his days in a wheelchair. His hands are twisted, and his feet won't support him. He can't feed himself. He can't comb his hair. He can't drive a car or play a game of tennis. He can't go for a walk. Yet he is a person of incredible faith and joy. Despite his challenges, he graduated from high school, he graduated from college, he taught in a junior college, he went on five overseas mission trips, and he became a missionary in Portugal. He went daily to a public park and talked to anybody who would listen about his Christian faith. He led seventy people to accept Christ as Lord and Savior.

He speaks from a wheelchair and holds a Bible in his lap. And just when people start to feel sorry for him, he holds his bent hand up in the air and says, "I have everything I need for joy" (Max Lucado, *The Applause of Heaven* [Dallas: Word Publishing, 1990], 6-7).

When we understand, really understand, how much God loves us and what God has done for us in Jesus Christ, we can't help but to "rejoice always," because no matter what happens to us, we know that God is with us and God is for us and God will always be there for us, come what may in this world and in the world to come. That's why we can rejoice always.

Second, Pray Without Ceasing

When Robert Louis Stevenson was a little boy, he once said to his mother, "Momma, you can't be good without praying."

"How do you know that, Robert?" she asked.

"Because I've tried," he answered.

This brings to mind another story about a little boy who had been sent to his room because he had misbehaved. A short time later, he came out and said to his mother, "Momma, I've been thinking about what I did, and I said a prayer."

"That's fine," she said, "If you ask God to help you be good, he will help you."

"Oh, I didn't ask him to help me be good," replied the little boy. "I asked him to help you put up with me!"

Sometimes we get so mixed up about prayer, the proper way to pray, the appropriate words to use, the correct physical posture for prayer.

Some say the only proper way to pray is on our knees. Others say we should pray with outstretched arms and with our eyes turned upward toward heaven. While others protest, "No! No! That posture is too proud. We should always pray with head bowed and eyes closed." Still others worry about how we should hold our hands when we pray or about whether there are special words we should use in a unique (even unusual) tone of voice when we communicate with God.

Now, when Paul said, "Pray without ceasing," that's not what he had in mind. He was not talking about pious words or flowery phrases or specific physical positions. No, he was talking about prayer being simply put, "Friendship with God." And we all know that a friend is one with whom we share the joys and sorrows of life.

Sometimes when I talk to young people about "relationships," I will say to them:

> Let me tell you who your friends are. Imagine that at 4:00 this afternoon you get a call telling you that someone has just given you twenty million dollars! Who would be the first two or three people you would want to share that good news with? That tells you who your friends are. Or, imagine that at 4:00 this afternoon instead of that call, you get a call telling you that someone you love dearly was just killed in a car wreck. Who would be the first person you would want to share that bad news with? That tells you who your friends are because your friends are those who laugh with you when you are happy and celebrate your joy, and they are those who cry with you and hold you up and support you when you are hurting.

As Christians, the first person we should think of in either of those scenarios is God because he is our best friend. He is the one to whom we can say, "Thank You, Lord," and he is the one to whom we can say, "Help me, Lord." And that's what it means to pray without ceasing, to share everything—everything—with God, to talk to him constantly about everything that's going on in our lives, not with pious words or sanctimonious phrases, but with simple words shared between best friends.

Now, let me say one more quick word about prayer. Our family has always believed strongly in prayer, but never more than now because of what we are experiencing as my wife, June, goes through her chemotherapy treatments. We are strengthened and encouraged and comforted as never before by our prayers and your prayers, by God's love and your love, by God's support and your support, by God's friendship and your friendship. We thank you and we thank God every single day, every single moment. That's what it means to "rejoice always," and to "pray without ceasing."

Third and Finally, Give Thanks in All Circumstances

Notice the preposition here is "in"—"*in* all circumstances," not "*for* all circumstances." We don't give thanks for cancer or car wrecks or heart attacks, but as Paul so well put it, we can give thanks in all circumstances because we can know that come what may, God is always with us, giving us the help we need. In his letter to the Philippians, Paul expressed it like this: "Bring it on! I'm ready for anything, for Christ is my strength."

At the 2004 United Methodist General Conference in Pittsburgh, one of the speakers was Randy Day. Randy is the General Secretary of the Board of Global Ministries, and in that job, he does a lot of international travel. Not too long ago, he and his wife adopted a little boy from another country, and the little boy has quickly become the delight of their house. When Randy Day travels, he always calls home from wherever he is. Once, he called from just across the International Dateline and told his young son, "It's dark where you are right now, but where I am it's light. In fact, it's tomorrow where I am."

Some months later, Randy had to leave home again, and as he said good-bye to his family, he said, "I'll call you when I get there," and his little boy said, "Dad, call me from tomorrow!"

That's why we can rejoice always and pray without ceasing and give thanks in all circumstances—because our Father God can call us from tomorrow.

He is the Lord of Life—yesterday, today, tomorrow, and forever. We can count on that and we can count on him because, although we may not know what the future holds, we know who holds the future.

And that's why we can rejoice always. We can pray without ceasing. And we can give thanks in all circumstances.

11

Rich in Mind, Body, and Spirit

Jesus Increased in Wisdom and in Stature and in Favor with God and People

Scripture: Luke 2:52

THERE IS AN INTERESTING STORY ABOUT SOMETHING THAT HAPPENED some years ago in our country. Two paddleboats left Memphis at about the same time. The two paddleboats were heading down the Mississippi River to New Orleans. As they traveled side by side, sailors from one of the boats began to make derogatory remarks about the slow pace of the other boat. Words were exchanged. Insults were shouted. Challenges were made. And the race began. The competition became vicious as the two boats roared through the Deep South.

One boat began falling behind. Not enough fuel. There had been plenty of coal for the normal trip, but not nearly enough for a fast and furious race. As the boat dropped back, an enterprising young sailor grabbed some of the ship's cargo and tossed it into the boat's ovens. When the other sailors on his boat saw what the young sailor was doing, and when they realized that the supplies burned as well as the coal, they got excited!

They quickly fueled their boat with the cargo they had been assigned to transport. Can you believe it? They ended up winning the race. But in the process, they burned up and lost all of their precious cargo!

Now, there is a sermon there somewhere because, you see, God has entrusted to us some special and precious cargo—our children,

79

our grandchildren, our spouses, our friends, our neighbors, our church, and our own souls. Our job is to do our part in seeing to it that this cargo entrusted to us reaches its intended destination.

But when the rat race and the rush to success become so furious and take priority over people (especially over the family), then people suffer and people get hurt. Think of it. How much precious cargo do we sacrifice in order to achieve the number one slot? How many people never reach their destinations because of the aggressiveness and the mixed-up priorities of a competitive captain?

Jesus warned us about this. He said, "What does it profit a man, a woman, a family, a nation . . . to gain the whole world and lose its own soul?" (paraphrase of Mark 8:36). What does it profit to win the rat race but lose your precious cargo in the process?

The point is clear. We must get back to emphasizing and promoting and cultivating the Christian home. It is urgent that we make the Christian home a top priority. Whether that home has nine people in it or one person in it, it is crucial that Christian faith and Christian virtues and Christian values are lived out there.

The Christian home should be the very first place where we learn not to be negative, but to celebrate life as a precious gift from God. The Christian home should be the very first place where we learn to love and learn that we are loved unconditionally. The Christian home should be the very first place we learn the difference between right and wrong. The Christian home should be the very first place we learn how to share and how to respect others. The Christian home should be the very first place we learn how to pray and hear the stories of Jesus. The Christian home should be the very first place we learn how to say yes to life, yes to other people, yes to the church, and yes to God.

Go to any prison today and interview the prisoners about how they ended up behind bars. You will find that the vast majority of the prison inmates (nine out of ten) will tell you that they came from dysfunctional families, that their problems root back to a bad situation at home, a destructive family. Let me hurry to say, though, this is not true for all of them! I personally know some situations in which the parents did everything right and still their child got into trouble. But most of the time—more than 90 percent of the time—the prisoners will say their problems root back to their early home life.

So the lesson for us is obvious. In the home:

🕊 Build your child's self-esteem.

🕊 Emphasize self-worth and self-respect.

🕊 Teach your children independent and wise decision-making.

🕊 Remind them constantly that they are special to you and special to God.

🕊 Teach them the Christian faith and the Christian lifestyle, but, more important, live your faith before them.

🕊 Keep them close to church and Sunday school and youth fellowship.

🕊 Teach them the scriptures.

🕊 Teach them to pray, but even better, let them see and hear you pray.

🕊 Make them dramatically aware of how much you and God and the church love them.

🕊 Most important of all, introduce them to Jesus Christ! Tell them the stories of Jesus, and let them see the spirit of Jesus Christ in you.

In Luke 2:52, we find a fascinating verse. Earlier in chapter 2, Luke has told the story of Jesus' birth, his presentation in the temple as a child, and the story of how as a young boy Jesus was left behind in Jerusalem accidentally and was found three days later by his parents. He was in the temple sitting and discussing theology with the scribes and elders. And then, Luke concludes the chapter with this sentence: "And Jesus increased in wisdom and in stature, and in favor with God and people" (paraphrase of NRSV). That is, he grew in mind, body, and spirit.

Not long ago, a woman in Tennessee celebrated her ninety-eighth birthday. She is still happy and healthy and sharp. Someone asked her what was her formula for such a long, happy, healthy, and productive life. She said, "Three things: think good thoughts, be kind to everybody, and eat prunes every day." Now, what she was saying was this:

She had taken care of her mind, her body, and her soul. That's our calling in the Christian home and the Christian church—to help children of all ages grow in mind, body, and spirit, increase in wisdom and in stature and in favor with God and people. Let's take a look at these one at a time.

First of All, We Help Our Children Grow in Wisdom (In Mind)

It's important to recognize that "book knowledge" and "wisdom" are not the same. Academic achievement and wisdom are two different things. I have known in my lifetime some people who were well educated and also very wise; but I have also known people who had no formal education at all, yet were amazingly wise.

Wisdom is not knowing all the answers on *Jeopardy* or solving the puzzle first on *Wheel of Fortune* or getting all the answers right on the final exam. According to the Bible, wisdom is the ability to know and understand God's will and the grace to do it. And you know, that's really what it means today, too, isn't it? And that's the main thing, the key thing, the crucial thing, we need to teach our children at home and in church.

At the United Methodist General Conference in Pittsburgh, the preacher of the day one morning was Bishop Robert Fannin. He told about something in his youth with which I really resonated. He said that before he came into the ministry he had a great and vast experience in the theater. He said he swept the floors, popped the popcorn, and sold the tickets; and that was the extent of his great experience in the theater.

He also said that as he worked in the theater in his hometown, they showed the same type of movie every Saturday—old Western movies in which the actors were different and the horses were different, but the story was the same. It was the good guys against the outlaws, and in the end, right would prevail and the good guys in the white hats would win.

Bishop Fannin went on to say that the one cowboy in those movies that he liked the most—the one he wanted to grow up to be like most of all—was the guy who rode out into the desert, got off his horse, knelt down, and put his hand and ear to the ground and said, "Two men approaching on horseback, riding out of the mountains, wearing six-shooters and carrying a rifle." Bishop Fannin said he admired that guy (the guide, the tracker) because he was always so cool and confident and composed. He was always so wise.

One Saturday, that character would be played by John Wayne, and the next Saturday Gary Cooper or Randolph Scott or Roy Rogers or Gene Autry would play the part. Whichever one it was, he was always so wise. He always knew what was coming, and he always knew just what to do to save the day. He was the tracker, the leader, the guide.

Don't you wish we had a guide like that today? Someone who could show us just the right thing to do, the wise thing to do, in every situation? Well, as a matter of fact, we have an even better tracker and leader and guide: his name is Jesus. He is the way, the truth, and the life. He is the Word of God, the Purpose of God, the Wisdom of God, wrapped up in a living person.

Some years ago, there was a great professor at Centenary College named Dean R. E. Smith. Dean Smith was a saintly man, a brilliant scholar, an outstanding communicator, and a real friend to the students. In one of his most famous lectures, Dean Smith talked to the students about how we discover truth and how we determine what is true and what is false.

After some discussion, Dean Smith suddenly asked the students this question: "How wide is my desk?" The students looked at the large desk and then made their best guesses. A variety of answers rang out. "I think it's about 72 inches wide." "No, I believe it's more like 68 inches wide." "Looks like 75 to me." Then some wise guy from the back of the room said, "71 5/16," and everybody laughed. Then Dean Smith said, "These are all pretty good guesses, but how do we figure out which one is most nearly true and accurate?" There was silence in the classroom for a moment, and then tentatively someone said, "Get a measuring stick?" "That's right," Dean Smith would say, "To determine which answer is closest to the truth, we have to get a measuring stick and measure."

Then Dean Smith went to the blackboard. He took a piece of chalk, and in silence, he drew the outline of a cross. With that piece of chalk, he traced over and over the sign of the cross, letting it dramatically sink into the hearts and minds of those students. Then, he stood back and pointed to that cross and said, "Ladies and gentlemen, there's your measuring stick! There's your measuring stick for truth!"

Now, look with me at that cross. There's our compass, our tracker, our guide. There's our measuring stick for truth. We can put our confidence in that. If the world tries to tell you that it's OK to take advantage of others for your own personal gain; if the world tries to tell you that it's not so bad to lie or cheat or hurt or steal or hold a grudge or hate, you just remember the cross. Remember the truth of Christ.

Everywhere we go these days, we see young people wearing necklaces with the letters *WWJD*. The letters stand for *What Would Jesus Do?* These young people are trying to measure their actions and their decisions by the truth of Christ, "What would Jesus do?"

The measuring stick of Christ tells us to be committed to God and compassionate toward one another; to be loving and caring and kind; to be just and honest and truthful; to be loyal and merciful and gracious. Anything that doesn't measure up to that is wrong and destructive and sinful! That's the best wisdom I know, and that's what we need to teach our children—to let Jesus Christ and his cross be the measuring stick for what is right and good and true. That's number one: we help our children grow in wisdom.

Second, We Help Our Children Grow in Stature (In Body)

Of course, in Luke 2, as we read that "Jesus increased in stature," it means that his body developed. He became taller and stronger. But also in the Bible, the word "body" often means more than our physical makeup. Quite often it means total personality, and sometimes the word "stature" means character. For example, if you hear a woman described like this: "She is a person of great stature in that community," we don't think of her physically. We don't think the woman is seven feet tall and weighs three hundred pounds. No, we think that she is a person noted and respected for her strength of character and influence and morality. It is so crucial that we teach our children the importance of honesty and integrity and ethical living.

Some time ago, *USA TODAY* ran an article about two cowboy churches in Texas ("Cowboy Church Rounds 'Em Up on Sunday,"

March 11, 2003). They printed the Cowboy's Ten Commandments. The writer of the *USA TODAY* article found the Cowboy's Ten Commandments posted on the wall at Cross Trails Church in Fairlie, Texas. The cowboys said they and their children could understand this version of the Ten Commandments better than the one with the "thou shalt nots" in it, and they said they could live up to them a lot better. The meaning is the same, but the words are "down-home Texas." Here they are, the Cowboy's Ten Commandments:

1. Just one God.
2. Honor yer Ma and Pa.
3. No telling tales or gossipin'.
4. Git yourself to Sunday meeting.
5. Put nothin' before God.
6. No foolin' around with another fellow's gal.
7. No killin'.
8. Watch yer mouth.
9. Don't take what ain't yers.
10. Don't be hankerin' for yer buddy's stuff.

Well, as we all know in Texas, cowboys just tell it like it is. However we tell it, we need to go to bed at night and get up in the morning and, in between, teach our children what's right and what's wrong, what's good and what's bad, what's just and what's unjust.

First, we help our children grow in wisdom, and second, we help our children grow in stature.

Third and Finally, We Help Our Children Grow in Favor with God and People (In Spirit, in Soul, in Relationships)

I like the story about a famous actor who was touring the country doing a one-man show in small towns to promote drama and the fine arts. One evening, he came to a small village, and everyone in town came out to see him and hear him. He was masterful, and at the end of his performance there was a long thunderous standing ovation. He had performed selections from Broadway, from Shakespeare, from movies, and from history; and the people were mesmerized by his incredible talent.

They applauded and cheered, and he came back onstage for an encore. He quieted the crowd and asked if anyone had a request. Seated on the front row was an older man who had been the pastor in that small village for over twenty years. The people all loved the elderly minister, and all turned to him to see if he had a request for the famous actor. The old pastor said, "I have a favorite, but our honored guest may not know it." "What is it?" the actor asked, and the elderly minister said, "The Twenty-third Psalm, the Shepherd's Psalm." The actor said, "I know it well, and I'll be glad to do it on one condition: that after I recite it, the minister will come and recite it, too."

At first the old minister tried to decline, saying he didn't feel worthy to be on the same stage with this world-famous actor. But the actor insisted, and the crowd called out for the minister to do it. So finally, but reluctantly, the pastor gave in and went up onstage.

The actor went first. He recited the Twenty-third Psalm with breathtaking eloquence. When he finished, there was a five-minute standing ovation. The older minister stood there in silence for a moment, thinking, "How in the world could I follow that?" But then he started thinking about how over the years God had been his Shepherd, and he began to quote the beautiful Shepherd's Psalm: "The Lord is my Shepherd, I shall not want." And when he finished, there was no applause, just holy and reverent silence. It was so powerful that tears filled the eyes of everyone in the auditorium. The actor walked over and put his arm around the shoulders of the old minister and said to the audience, "My friends, did you notice that there was a difference in the way the two of us recited the Twenty-third Psalm?" The actor paused for a moment and then said, "The difference was this: I know the Shepherd's Psalm, but he knows the Shepherd!"

Let me ask you something: Do you know the Shepherd? Do you know him, really? Do your children know him? It is so important, so crucial, so urgent to help our children grow in mind, body, and spirit, to grow in wisdom and in stature and in favor with God and people.

12

Rich in the Risen Christ

When the Risen Christ Comes Looking for Us

Scripture: John 21:15-19

O<small>N</small> N<small>OVEMBER</small> 1, 1972, <small>OUR FAMILY LEFT</small> W<small>EST</small> T<small>ENNESSEE AND</small> moved to Shreveport, Louisiana, so I could join the staff of the First United Methodist Church there as the preaching associate. For the next twelve years, I had the distinct, unique, and amazing experience of working side by side daily with Dr. D. L. Dykes.

Dr. Dykes was without question one of the greatest preachers I have ever heard, one of the most creative and innovative leaders I have ever known, and one of the most lovingly colorful and eccentric personalities I have ever met. He was a legend in his own time. He had been on television in that area (on the CBS affiliate station) for twenty years, and everybody in the Ark-La-Tex region of our country knew him. Everybody from the smallest child to the oldest adult affectionately called him "D. L."

D. L. was known far and wide for his driving. One time when I was in his car with him, the Shreveport police pulled us over. The patrolman walked up to the car, leaned over, looked in, and said, "Aw shucks, D. L. It's just you. Go on. I didn't recognize your new car."

The very first time I went anywhere with him in his car, he wanted to stop at the print shop in downtown Shreveport. When we got there, D. L. went around the block once, but there were no parking places near the print shop. So he just jumped the curb and parked on the sidewalk in front of the print shop's main door! He jumped out, left the car engine running, asked me to stay there and watch the car, and ran into the print shop.

I was new to Shreveport and didn't know what to do, except sit there and pray that the police wouldn't come by. I felt like the lookout in the getaway car. Well, before I could even get that prayer out, the police did come by. The policeman said, "Is this your car?" I said, "No, sir." "Whose car is it?" he asked. I said, "It belongs to Dr. D. L. Dykes." And the policeman said, "This is D. L.'s car?" "Yes, sir." "Well, OK," he said, "but tell him next time it would probably be best if he parked on the street." "Yes, sir," I said with a sigh of relief.

As well known as D. L. was for his driving, he was even more famous for his eloquent, powerful, conversational preaching. He never raised his voice. He just stood in the pulpit and talked in a conversational tone. He could hold a congregation in the palm of his hand because all of the people in the sanctuary, and those watching on TV, felt strongly that D. L. was speaking directly, personally, intimately, and individually to each one of them.

D. L. was a fantastic storyteller, and when he would tell a personal story about something that had happened to him in his early life, you were there with him. With his word, he could transport you back in time to that little house where he grew up in Pleasant Hill, Louisiana, and the story would be so vivid, so powerful, that you could smell the soup his mother was cooking in the kitchen!

But as eloquent as D. L. was, one Sunday morning he got his tongue twisted and could not get out what he wanted to say. He was telling a story about a man he knew who had an interesting way of dealing with his problems. He would write his problems on a card on Friday afternoon and then place that card in a desk drawer. The man didn't want to take his problems home with him for the weekend. He didn't want his problems to be a burden to him and his family over the weekend, so he would leave the card with the problems written on it in a desk drawer. Then on the following Monday morning, he would take the card out and deal with the problems the best he could.

That's what he meant to say, but on that fateful Sunday morning with twelve hundred people in church and thousands more watching on television, here's what happened: He said, "I know this man who has a desk in his drawers." The congregation snickered at first and then laughed loudly. D. L. turned to me and said, "What did I say?" I answered, "You said you know a man who has a desk in his drawers." D. L. laughed and said, "That's not what I meant to say. I meant to say, I know a man who has a desk in his drawers." The congregation roared again even more loudly. D. L. turned to me and said, "Did I do it again?" I said, "Yes, sir." He tried again and again and again—five times—and he never did get it right. But then, as only D. L. could do, he rose to the occasion and said, "Is there anybody here who has any idea what I'm trying to say?" And the congregation laughed again.

Now, the point is: it happens to the best of us. We can all get into trouble with our words. Sometimes we say the wrong things and our words come back to haunt us!

Have you heard about the mother who invited some people to dinner? At the table, she turned to her six-year-old daughter and said, "Would you like to say the blessing?" The little girl replied, "I wouldn't know what to say." The mother insisted. "You can do it, honey. Just say what you hear Mommy say." The little girl bowed her head, closed her eyes, and said, "Lord, what on earth was I thinking when I invited all these people to dinner?"

This is what happened to Simon Peter on the night before Jesus was crucified. His words spoken in haste that fateful night in a moment of braggadocio came back to weigh heavily on his heart, and it thrust him into despair. Go back with me to that poignant scene.

Jesus and his disciples had just finished the Last Supper in the Upper Room. They sang a hymn and then went out to the Mount of Olives. There, Jesus told his disciples that they were fast approaching the showdown, and in that crunch moment, they would all fall away. They would all deny him, they would all forsake him. But boldly, Peter said to Jesus, "Not me, Lord. All the rest of them may fall away but not me. You can count on me. I would never fail you. I would never deny you. I will go with you to prison and even to death. The others may become weak in the crisis, but not me. I will stand tall. That, you can count on." And Jesus said, "Simon, Simon, I know you mean well, but the truth is that this very night before the cock crows twice, you will deny me three times" (paraphrase of Matthew 26:33-34).

And of course, Jesus was right. That is precisely what happened. Peter was emotionally and spiritually devastated by his failure to live up to his bold words. How could he face Christ again after falling on his face so completely? How could he be a trusted leader of the disciple group ever again after his colossal collapse? How could he ever speak again about his commitment to Christ and expect anybody to believe him? How could he redeem himself?

Well, the fact is, he couldn't redeem himself, but Christ could! The risen Lord could redeem him and forgive him and encourage him and give him a new lease on life, and that is precisely what this wonderful story in John 21 is all about.

Christ resurrects, and then the risen Lord comes looking for Simon Peter. He knows full well that Simon Peter had failed that night, not once, not twice, but three times. And the risen Christ knows how heartsick Simon Peter must be. He knows that Peter needs forgiveness, needs reassurance, needs a new chance and a new life. So the risen Christ comes to meet him where he is and to give him what he needs.

This is the good news of Easter and the Christian faith for you and me. This great story shows us that Christ not only can conquer evil and death, but he also can resurrect us. He did that for Simon Peter that day. He can do it for you and me this day. That's what John 21 teaches us.

Who could ever forget that scene? After the risen Christ serves the disciples breakfast (another Holy Communion), he looks Simon Peter square in the eye and asks him the same question three times: "Simon, do you love me?" "Oh yes, Lord," Simon answers, "you know I love you." "Then, feed my sheep," the Risen Lord says to him. "Feed my sheep!" (paraphrase of John 21:15-17).

Of course, it's obvious what's going on here. Christ is forgiving Peter and giving him a chance to profess his love three times to make up for his earlier threefold denial. Then the story ends exactly the way it started months before with Christ saying to Simon at the seashore these two powerful words: "Follow me." Notice this now. The first thing and the last thing Jesus said to Simon Peter was that simple command: "Follow me."

Isn't that a great story, jam-packed with the stuff of life, powerful symbols, strong emotions, dramatic lessons? One of the key lessons for us today is to see how the risen Christ seeks out Simon Peter and meets his need and how he does that for us too. He seeks us out; he comes looking for us to meet our needs.

In Simon Peter's experience with Christ back then, we get a practical glimpse at three of the powerful ways the risen Christ meets us and helps us today. Let me show you what I mean.

First of All, When We Most Need Love, the Risen Christ Comes to Love Us

Recently, I ran across a story that touched me deeply. It was a busy morning in the doctor's office. Just a few minutes after eight, a gentleman in his eighties showed up to have some stitches removed from his thumb. He told the nurse that he was in a big hurry because he had an important appointment at 9:00 that morning and must not be late.

The nurse took his vital signs and had him take a seat, knowing it would be over an hour before anyone would be able to see him. The nurse noticed that the man kept looking at his watch urgently, and she decided to see if she could help the man. She looked at his injured thumb, and it looked good. It was healing nicely. She reported this to the doctor, and he told her to remove his stitches and to re-dress his thumb. As she was doing this, she and the older man got into a nice conversation. "So you have an urgent appointment at 9:00 this morning?" she said. "Yes," he said, "the same appointment I have every morning. Every morning at 9:00 I go to the nursing home to have breakfast with my wife." The nurse smiled and said, "You are such a handsome gentleman. I bet that's the highlight of her day." The man blinked and said, "She doesn't know who I am. She has had Alzheimer's disease for quite a while. She hasn't recognized me in the last five years." The nurse was surprised, and she said, "And you still go every morning, even though she doesn't know who you are?" The man smiled, patted the nurse's hand, and said, "She doesn't know who I am, but I know who she is."

There's a word for that. It's called *love*—unwavering, unshakeable, unconditional love. And that's the kind of love Jesus Christ had for

Simon Peter. He knew who Simon Peter was, and he knew how Simon Peter must be feeling. He knew that Simon Peter the Rock had crumbled and how he felt like dirt!

So here came the risen Lord to give Simon Peter the encouragement, the affirmation, the reassurance, the love he needed so much in that moment. No "I told you so's" here. No stern lectures here. No fanning the flames of guilt here. No blame-placing or finger-pointing here. Just words of love.

In this powerful and touching breakfast scene, Jesus, the risen Christ, is saying to Simon Peter: "I still love you. I still trust you. I still believe in you. I know you can do it. I want you to lead out. I want you to take up the torch of my ministry. I want you to take care of my sheep. I want you to watch over my flock."

Now, we know that these words of love became the wake-up call Simon Peter needed. As we read on in the scriptures, we see how he became one of the courageous leaders and martyrs of the early church.

The point for us is obvious. Just as the risen Christ came to Peter that day with the words and acts of love he so desperately needed, that's the way he comes to us, with unwavering, unshakeable, unconditional love. That's number one. When we most need love, the risen Christ comes to love us.

Second, When We Most Need Forgiveness, the Risen Christ Comes to Forgive Us

Simon Peter needed forgiveness, and that is precisely what Christ came to give him.

It happened in the early 1970s. Her name was Teresa. She was sixteen years old and having a hard time growing up. One Friday night, she had an ugly fight with her parents. She ran away from home and stayed away for almost two years. Her parents searched desperately for her but with no luck. Finally, they hired a detective. The detective brought back a sordid story that I couldn't even begin to describe in the polite pulpit. Teresa had done everything a girl could do that would break her parents' hearts—drugs, alcohol, life in a promiscuous commune, participating in all kinds of illicit activity.

Then one morning (it was Good Friday), the phone rang in my office. It was a collect call from Teresa. She was calling from San Francisco. She was crying. "Oh, Jim," she said, "I have done everything wrong. I have hurt my parents so much. Now I realize how foolish I have been. I want to come home, but I don't know if Mom and Dad want me back. I wouldn't blame them if they didn't. I don't know how they could ever forgive me. I'm so sorry. I want to come home." I told her to go to the airport and give her name at the airline desk. I would have a ticket home waiting there for her, and someone would be at the local airport to meet her plane.

When she got off the plane on that Good Friday afternoon, she looked pretty rough. Her hair was dirty and matted. Her clothes were rumpled and threadbare. Her eyes were tired and bloodshot. Her parents rushed to her and hugged her and welcomed her home with love and grace while crying tears of joy and relief.

Two days later on Easter Sunday morning, they were in church together. Teresa sat between her mom and dad. She looked like a new person. She was radiant and beautiful. All through the service, her parents kept touching her, patting her, hugging her. After the service, they came down to speak to me. As Teresa's mother hugged me tightly, she whispered in my ear, "Jim, I've always believed in the resurrection, but never more than right now!"

Through the power of God's amazing grace, we can work miracles when we, in the spirit of the risen Christ, reach out to others with forgiveness. When we need it most, the risen Christ comes looking for us with love and forgiveness.

Third and Finally, When We Most Need Direction, the Risen Christ Comes to Direct Us

Simon Peter and the other disciples had been waiting around, wondering, "What next? What are we supposed to do now?" Then the risen Christ came to give them a new direction. He said, "If you love me, then feed my sheep." What he meant was, "Take up the torch of my ministry! Go! Be the church for this needy world!" The world is starving to death for Jesus Christ and we have him. Our task is to feed his sheep, to share him with others.

I have a good friend who is one of the most outgoing, gregarious persons I have ever known. He is so full of life that he just lights up the room. Physically, he is a great big guy—a former football player, strong, powerful—and yet he has a teddy bear personality. He is a hugger. He just hugs everybody; he is wired up that way. He expresses his love with hugs.

Some years ago, I heard him speak to a group of young people, and he said something that inspired them and touched me. He said, "When I first became a Christian, I was so frustrated because I wanted to hug God and didn't know how." He said, "I was so thrilled by what God had done for me in Christ. I was so grateful for the way God had turned my life around, I wanted to hug God, but I didn't know how." And then he said this: "Over the years, I have learned that the best way to hug God is to hug his children; the best way to love God is to love his children; the best way to serve God is to serve his children."

He's right, you know. That's precisely what the risen Christ was saying to Peter that day. If you love me, then feed my sheep and take care of my flock. That's the direction I want you to take. That's exactly what I want you to do.

Now, let me tell you something. The risen Christ is here with us today. He is here right now. He has come to give us the love, the forgiveness, and the direction we so desperately need.

13

Rich in Easter Faith

Jesus and Mary Magdalene

Scripture: John 20:11-18

T HEN CAME SUNDAY MORNING, *EASTER SUNDAY MORNING!*
While it was still dark, Mary Magdalene went to the tomb. She saw immediately that the stone had been rolled away from the cave's entrance and that the grave was empty. Alarmed, Mary ran to find Simon Peter and John. Together, they ran back to the grave site and found it just as Mary had described it, the stone pushed back and the tomb empty.

Peter and John turned back toward home, trying to sort out what on earth this could mean, but Mary, so crestfallen, stayed there in the garden just outside the tomb to grieve and mourn alone. She wept softly. She thought someone had stolen Jesus' body. She wondered aloud: *How could they do this? Haven't they done enough? And now this. They have stolen his body. They have hidden it from us. Have they no shame? Have they no feelings at all?*

Then, in what some have called the greatest recognition scene in all of history, Mary suddenly ran head-on into the Resurrection. She suddenly recognized the risen Lord! At first, she thought that he was the gardener, but when he called her name, "Mary," her eyes were opened to the truth of Easter. She saw firsthand the risen Christ. And as always happens when we encounter the living Lord up close and personal, he put her to work. He gave her a job. He sent her to tell the good news to the others.

Mary ran as fast as her excited feet could carry her to find the other disciples, laughing and shouting the good news of Easter. "He is risen! He is risen. I have seen the Lord! Christ is risen!"

Isn't that a great story? If that story doesn't make you tingle all over with excitement, then you had better check your spiritual pulse.

William Sangster was one of the great preachers of the twentieth century. Toward the end of his life, he became quite ill. His vocal chords were paralyzed, and he was unable to speak. On the Easter Sunday morning just before he died, he painfully printed a short note to his daughter. In it he wrote these poignant words: "How terrible to wake up on Easter and have no voice to shout, 'He is risen!' but it is far worse to have a voice and not want to shout."

Let me ask you something: do you want to shout? Do you want to run and tell the whole wide world the good news of Easter? The good news that ultimately God wins! That the eternal goodness of God overcomes the evil Golgothas of history. This is the amazing, incredible, exciting message of Easter. On Good Friday, evil had its best chance to defeat God and could not do it. Christ conquered death. He came out of the grave! God won the victory, and he wants to share the Easter victory with you and me by giving us some very special Easter gifts.

Let me share three of those with you. Forgive me for being so personal, but I want to underscore for us three special Easter gifts that have become even more real to my wife, June, and me because of what we have been going through in recent times.

First of All, Easter Gives Us a Sense of Peace

Mary Magdalene came trudging to the tomb that morning, brokenhearted, scared, worried, confused, troubled, frightened. But there at the garden tomb, the resurrected Christ gave her a great sense of victory and confidence and peace.

In 2004, my wife, June, and I experienced two Good Fridays. One was with the whole world as we remembered the sacrificial love of Jesus Christ and how he gave his life for us on the cross of Calvary.

The other Good Friday was a personal one for us. It came two weeks earlier. June had been experiencing some physical symptoms that sent us to the doctor. We fully expected the doctor to change her diet or prescribe some miracle medicine that would just fix her up in no time. That's what we expected, but it was not what we got.

After a brief examination, the doctor, who is a good friend of ours, said, "It's 2:30. I will be here at the hospital until at least 6:00. Let's get some blood work and a CT scan." Then he added, "I want to read the CT scan before I go home because I want to talk to you face to face and not call you on the phone with the results."

An alarm went off in our heads. At 6:30 that evening, the doctor came back with the report. Suddenly that Friday evening became different from any other we had ever experienced. The CT scan confirmed what the doctor had feared, that June had a tumor in her abdominal region and it needed to come out quickly. It was like an out-of-body experience for us. All of a sudden, we were hearing words like *major surgery, oncology, blockage,* and *chemotherapy.*

We were checked into the hospital, and our great Methodist Hospital began immediately to make the necessary preparations to assemble a world-class team of doctors and to arrange for the emergency surgery. The surgery took place the following Tuesday morning and went into the afternoon. Finally the doctors came out to tell us that the surgery had gone as planned, that June had withstood the surgery well, but that as they had expected, she had ovarian cancer, and chemotherapy would be necessary.

Later that afternoon, the children and I went in to see June in ICU, and we told her the full story. The doctors also came and described the situation and answered all of her questions. She handled it all with grace and poise and courage. Late that night, I went back to ICU alone to say good night to June. We held hands and had a prayer, and then June said some words I will never, ever forget. She said, "When I was a little girl, we used to sing a song in Sunday school that had the words, 'I've got the peace that passes understanding down in my heart.' I just loved that song, but I really didn't know what that meant back then. I know tonight exactly what it means. I don't understand what's happening in my body, but I prayed to God that he would give me peace. And he has! Even with all that I have been through and all I have yet to go through, I have this deep sense of peace that passes understanding."

And I said, "That's because of all the prayers that are being prayed for you right now, and it's because God is right here with us." And June said, "I know. I can feel his presence here and I'm not afraid. I just feel so peaceful."

A few days later, June received a get-well card from some dear friends, and that card summed it up perfectly. It read:

> May the hands that formed the earth touch your body and heal it
> May the breath that moved over the waters fill your soul with life.
> May the heart that sacrificed to save you surround your heart with comfort.
> May knowing that you are in the hands of an all-powerful, all-loving God bring you peace.

This is the good news of Easter. God wins! He has conquered Death! Good Fridays are always followed by Easter Sundays! God is still in charge! God is on both sides of the grave! God's love is the most powerful thing in the world, and he loves *us*! And when we understand that, when we embrace that and wrap our arms around that and give our hearts to that, then we have the peace that passes understanding. That's the first gift that Easter gives us—a sense of peace.

Second, Easter Gives Us a Sense of Humor

When I think about Mary Magdalene running back to tell the others the good news on that Easter Sunday morning, I picture her running and jumping and shouting and laughing! Proverbs 31 has an amazing line. The writer is describing what it means to be a good wife and mother, and we find here these fascinating words: "Strength and dignity are her clothing, and she laughs at the time to come" (v. 25).

Notice that last phrase, "She laughs at the time to come." When I was a young Christian, I had no idea what on earth that could mean, but over the years, I have come to love that line because it means that people of faith have no fear of the future, no fear of what lies ahead, no fear even of death. Because as Christians, we can know that, come what may, we are never far from God's grace. Come what may, God loves us and will be there for us. So we don't have to run scared; we can have, because of Easter, a great sense of humor.

June's sense of humor has served her well through this ordeal. On the Saturday morning after the CT scan, just the two of us were in June's hospital room. I was thinking deep thoughts, trying to digest the heavy news we had received the night before. Pensively, I said, "June, I was just thinking, with all we've got to face, maybe I should just go on and retire and then I could be there all day, every day, just to take care of you." And she said, "Well, I was just thinking that with all we've got to face and all it's going to cost, you may need to work ten more years!" And we had a good laugh.

On another occasion, she said, "The doctors say that one good thing I have going for me is that I am in great health. Sure," she laughed, "I have a tumor, but other than that, I'm in great health!"

June's birthday was April Fool's Day, just two days after her surgery. Her surgeon came into her hospital room early that morning and said to her, "June, has anybody played an April Fool's joke on you yet?" And she said to him, "Just you!"

It's so important, so healthy, so crucial, so Christian, so Easter to have a good sense of humor because we know that God has already won the victory, and through faith in him, we can have the victory too. We can have strength, dignity, poise, confidence, and joy; and we can laugh at the time to come. We can laugh, come what may, because with God on our side, we cannot lose. In his own good time and in his own gracious way, in the world and in the world to come, he will give us the victory. First, Easter gives us a sense of peace, and, second, Easter gives us a sense of humor.

Third and Finally, Easter Gives Us a Sense of Mission

When we really come face to face with the risen Christ, he puts us to work, he gives us a job, he sends us on a mission. This is what he did for Mary. He gave her a sense of mission on that first Easter morning. He told her to go and tell the good news of his resurrection to his followers, to go tell the world the amazing story of his incredible victory.

Two nights before June's surgery, our family came to be with us. Our daughter, Jodi, and her husband, Danny; and our son, Jeff, and his wife, Claire, drove down from Dallas; and they brought all four of our grandchildren—Sarah, 10; Paul, 7; Dawson, 4; and Daniel, 2. It was great! They were all so loving and so affectionate. We have a neat picture of all four of them lying side by side on June's hospital bed watching *Scooby-Doo* on television.

It was so interesting. Every few minutes a nurse would come into the room to see if we needed anything. After this happened four or five times, we realized that two-year-old Daniel, who loves to push buttons, was pushing the red Nurse Call Button on the hospital bed!

It was about then that our daughter-in-law, Claire, decided to take all four children for a walk in the hospital. As they left the room, Jodi said to her daughter, Sarah, who is the oldest of the four grandchildren: "Sarah, you help with the little boys." And Sarah said, "Momma, that's why I'm here!"

Sarah was right, wasn't she? Helping one another, loving one another, taking care of one another—that's why we are here. That is our Easter mission.

Easter has some very special gifts for us. Easter gives us hope, forgiveness, salvation, and eternal life; and it gives us a sense of peace, a sense of humor, and a sense of mission.

14

Rich in Commitment to Christ

Jesus and Bartimaeus

Scripture: Mark 10:46-52

It happened almost twenty years ago. I had been at St. Luke's for only a few months. It was a beautiful spring day. The phone rang in our home on a Sunday afternoon. I answered, and a young man on the other end of the line said he needed to tell me something and then ask me a question. The words came in a rush of emotion. He told me that a month ago, he was in our church and felt God touching his heart and urging him to come down front to be baptized and join the church. "It was so powerful," he said. "I knew God was there calling me to do this, but," he said, "I procrastinated when time came to join. I felt strongly that I should come forward, but I was in the balcony in the middle of a crowded pew. I began to think of all the reasons not to come. I was so far away from the front. I might disturb other people trying to get out into the aisle. I might not get there in time. So I just grabbed hold of the back of the pew and held on for dear life. Then it was too late. The service ended." He said, "I walked out of the church so disgusted with myself. I knew deep in my heart that God wanted me to come down and make my commitment to Christ and the church, and I had fought it off."

The man went on to describe how disappointed he was with himself and how much he regretted letting that special moment pass, and then he said, "I promised God that if I ever felt that way again, I would seize that moment and act upon it boldly. I promised God I would do that." He paused for a moment, and then with some embarrassment he said, "It happened again this morning. It happened again. God touched my heart in church this morning, and I'm so ashamed to tell you that I did the same thing as before. I grabbed hold of the pew and fought it off again and did nothing. And I have been miserable all afternoon. I'm so mad at myself." And then he said, "Jim, just before I called you, I said a prayer and told God how bad I feel that he gave me two special moments and I turned away from both of them. I made a promise to God that I intend to keep. I promised God that I was going to get baptized before the sun goes down tonight. Jim, here is the question: will you baptize me before the sun goes down tonight?"

I said, "Of course I will." Then he said, "I forgot to mention it, but I promised God I would get baptized by immersion!" He said, "I feel so dirty because of how I failed twice before; I want to be washed clean. I want to be immersed!"

"Well, you know," I said to him, "I will have to make arrangements. I'll need to call Bethany Christian or River Oaks Baptist to see if we could use their baptistery. They may have services going on. We may have to wait till tomorrow, and . . ."

"Jim," he said, interrupting my ramblings, "I don't think you heard me." "Pardon me?" He said, "I promised God that I would be baptized by immersion before the sun goes down tonight. I would like for you to do it, but if you can't do it, I'll find somebody else who will."

Still trying to figure out just how to handle this and help this young man, I said, "Well, I do want to baptize you, I would be honored, but I'm trying to figure out the best way to get this done this afternoon." And he said, "Don't y'all have a swimming pool down there at the church?" "Well, as a matter of fact, yes, we do." "What's wrong with that?" he asked, and I said, "Nothing! Meet me at the pool at 5:00 p.m."

As I drove to the church, however, all these worries and questions were running through my head:

🐟 Is it OK to baptize somebody in a swimming pool?

🐟 What did they teach me in seminary about this? I couldn't remember this ever coming up.

🍂 What does the *Discipline* of our church say about this?

🍂 I'm new to the Texas Conference. Will they kick me out for doing this?

🍂 My goodness, what if the bishop finds out about this? What will he say to me or do to me over this?

I had all these haunting questions until I saw that young man standing there by the pool, waiting for me. I'll never forget the look on his face. The commitment, the urgency, the passion, the gratitude, the relief, the determination, the intensity, the resolve in his face. It was incredible! And I thought to myself as I greeted him, "I don't know what the letter of the law of the church says about this, but I do know one thing: I know what Jesus would do." And that's what I did. I met him where he was and baptized him. As I asked him the baptism profession of faith questions, it was amazing. He was so excited, I could hardly get the questions out before he would answer with great enthusiasm.

"Do you accept Jesus Christ as the Lord and Savior of your life?" "Yes I do! Absolutely, I do! Oh man, do I ever!"

"Do you accept the truths of God?" "Yes."

"Do you promise to live a Christian life?" "Yes."

And on and on with the questions, and then finally I said, "Do you want to be baptized in this faith?" And he said, "Absolutely! Absolutely! Yes, I do! Yes, I do!" I took his hand, prayed a prayer, led him down into the pool and baptized him, and received him into the church. It was a beautiful moment, and I felt the presence of God there with us.

Now, let me hurry to say that I don't recommend this. It's best to be baptized in the sanctuary with the whole church family participating. I'd never done it before, and I've never done it since, but for that young man on that particular day, that's what he needed.

By the way, the very next Sunday morning, he came down at the end of the 11:00 service to make his public profession of faith in Christ as his Lord and Savior. And he became a very active and effective member of our church.

Now, to this moment, when I think of that young man and his unshakeable determination that day, he reminds me of Bartimaeus.

In this powerful story in Mark 10, we see dramatically that even though Bartimaeus was blind, he saw vividly this "once in a lifetime" opportunity he had coming up as Jesus approached.

Somebody sent me an e-mail message last week telling about a young husband and wife on a TV talk show. The young man was asked, "What is your wife's favorite flower?" And he said, "I'm not sure, but I think it's Pillsbury!" The e-mail ended with these words, "And from that point things got ugly!" That left-brained young husband was not very sensitive, was he? But Bartimaeus was. He was sensitive to the uniqueness of this moment as Jesus walked by. Remember the story with me.

Jesus was on his way to Jerusalem. He was on his way to the cross when he encountered this man, Bartimaeus. Bartimaeus, who was blind, was sitting by the roadside in Jericho, doing what he did daily—begging for money. Obviously, he had heard about Jesus. Bartimaeus sensed strongly that this was his moment, his chance. So when Jesus came near, Bartimaeus began to cry out urgently, "Jesus, Son of David, have mercy on me!" The crowd tried to shush him. They thought Jesus was too busy and too important to be bothered with the likes of Bartimaeus, this poor, wretched, blind beggar. But Bartimaeus would not be denied. He would not be shushed. He cried out more desperately, "Son of David, have mercy on me!" Suddenly, Jesus stopped. He turned around. Somehow, amazingly, over the noise of the crowd, Jesus heard the urgent cry of Bartimaeus, and Jesus called for him. "Bartimaeus! Bartimaeus," the people said, "get up, he is calling for you." Then Bartimaeus threw his cloak aside. He sprang up and made his way through the crowd into the presence of Jesus.

Notice how gracious Jesus was with him. Jesus was not presumptuous or arrogant or controlling. Humbly, gently, Jesus asked, "What would you like me to do for you?" And Bartimaeus answered, "My teacher, let me see again." Then Jesus said to him, "Go your way; your faith has made you well." The scriptures tell us that the blind man, Bartimaeus, then received his sight. And listen to this: he *followed* Jesus on the way.

What a great story this is, great drama, great characters, great theology, and great lessons to learn here! Let me lift up three great lessons we discover in this story, the lessons of grit, grace, and gratitude.

First, There Is the Lesson of Grit

If you look up the word "grit" in a thesaurus, you will find there these synonyms: *gutsy, bravery, stamina, backbone, pluck, fortitude.* The meaning of the word "grit" comes into even sharper focus when we look at the antonyms, or the opposites: *timidity, fearfulness, faintheartedness, cold feet.* So for the purposes now, let me define the word like this: Grit is the courage to sense and seize the moment. And that is exactly what Bartimaeus did!

Bartimaeus's special qualities jump out of this story: his persistence, his boldness, his perseverance, his determination, his awareness of the power of this moment, his faith, his unwillingness to give in to the fear of embarrassment, his intense understanding (like the young man at the swimming pool) *that it's now or never for me.* All of these great attributes are found in Bartimaeus's true grit.

Let me tell you a story about a young man named Jerry, who is a great example of the spirit of grit. Jerry is one of those guys who is always in a good mood and always has something positive to say. Ask him how he is doing and he always says, "If I were any better I would be twins." Someone once asked him why he was always so upbeat, and Jerry said, "Each morning I wake up and say to myself, 'Jerry, you have two choices today. You can choose to be in a good mood, or you can choose to be in a bad mood.' Each time something bad happens, I can choose to be a victim, or I can choose to learn from it. I choose to learn from it. I choose the positive side of life. Life is all about choices. When you cut away all the junk, every situation is a choice. You choose how you react to situations. You choose how people affect your mood. The bottom line: It's your choice how you live life, and I choose to live and be positive and to celebrate life."

Jerry was the manager of a restaurant. One morning he was held up at gunpoint by three armed robbers. While trying to open the safe, his nervous hand slipped off the combination. The robbers panicked and shot him. Luckily, Jerry was found quickly and rushed to the trauma center. Jerry said that when he saw the sad expressions on the faces of the doctors and nurses, he read in their eyes the fear that "this man is a goner!" Jerry knew he had to take action, so when they asked him if he was allergic to anything, he said, "Yes, I'm allergic to bullets!" As the medical team laughed, Jerry said, "I am choosing to live, so operate on me as if I am alive, not dead."

After eighteen hours of surgery and weeks of intensive care, Jerry was released from the hospital with fragments of bullets still in his body. Everywhere he went, when people asked how he was doing, Jerry would answer, "If I were any better, I would be twins. Want to see my scars?"

Jerry lived, thanks to the skill of those great doctors and nurses, but also thanks to his faith and determination and grit.

Let me ask you something: do you have that kind of positive determination? Do you have the kind of true grit that Jerry had and Bartimaeus had and the young man at the swimming pool had? That's lesson number one we learn from the Bartimaeus story: the lesson of grit.

Second, There Is the Lesson of Grace

The Bartimaeus story is jammed-full of amazing grace, the saving, healing, redemptive, eye-opening, life-changing power of God's miraculous and gracious love.

One of the outstanding preachers in our nation today is a young United Methodist minister named Tyrone Gordon. He followed Zan Holmes at St. Luke's in Dallas. Recently, I had the wonderful privilege of leading a national workshop on preaching with Tyrone. He is a delight. He said that when he first got out of seminary, he wanted to show everybody how educated he was, so in his first appointment after graduating from theological school, every Sunday he would quote great theologians such as Karl Barth, Paul Tillich, Rudolph Bultmann, and Reinhold Niebuhr. After several Sundays of that, Tyrone said, "Sister Jones pulled me aside and said, 'Tyrone, we don't care about all of that. Just tell us about Jesus.'"

Sister Jones was right, wasn't she? We don't really need to know about existentialism and eschatology. All we need to know about is

Jesus and his amazing grace. All we need to know about is Jesus and his power to give us the miracle of a new life, a new start, a new chance, and a new vision.

Isn't it beautiful here in Mark 10 how Jesus not only heals Bartimaeus and restores his sight, but also does it so tenderly, so graciously. Everybody else considered Bartimaeus to be an outcast and a lowlife, but Jesus treated him with love and dignity and respect. There's a name for that. It's called *grace*. That's the second lesson we learn from this great story.

Third and Finally, There Is the Lesson of Gratitude

Bartimaeus was so grateful for what Jesus did for him, he just dropped everything and followed Jesus, which, by the way, is the biblical way for saying Bartimaeus became a disciple of Jesus.

Our son, Jeff, and his beautiful wife, Claire, were married on April 12, 1996. On the night before their wedding, at the rehearsal dinner, Jeff said something I will never forget. After dinner, he stood up to thank everybody. His very first sentence moved everyone in the banquet hall. He said, "If I lived thirty lifetimes, I could never repay my family for what they have done for me."

All of us in the room were moved to tears by his gratitude. And you know, if you blow it up a bit, that's the same kind of gratitude I feel today toward Jesus Christ. If I lived thirty lifetimes or fifty lifetimes or one hundred lifetimes, I could never repay Jesus for what he has done for me.

I have a wonderful life, a great family, and a meaningful career all because of Jesus.

I have a sense of purpose, a sense of calling, a sense of fulfillment, and a sense of mission in my heart all because of Jesus.

Jesus gave to Bartimaeus a new life, a new chance, a new start, a new vision, and a new hope; and he gave me all those things, too.

So, like Bartimaeus, in gratitude, I chose to follow Jesus, to give my heart and soul to him, to commit my life to him. Let me ask you something. Have you made that decision yet? Do you feel so grateful to Jesus Christ for what he has done for you that you have chosen to follow him? That's what this great story of Bartimaeus is about. That's what the Christian faith is about. It's about grit, grace, and gratitude. When you have that kind of commitment to Christ—a commitment of grit, grace, and gratitude—then you are rich indeed, rich in the things that count the most!

Suggestions for Leading a Study of
Rich in the Things That Count the Most

John D. Schroeder

In this book, author James W. Moore shows how true fulfillment, true "wealth," comes from knowing God is with us, and the author encourages us to think about the riches in our lives that will last and endure. To assist you in facilitating a discussion group, this study guide was created to help make this experience beneficial for both you and members of your group. Here are some thoughts on how you can help your group:

1. Distribute the book to participants before your first meeting and request that they come having read the first chapter. You may want to limit the size of your group to increase participation.
2. Begin your sessions on time. Your participants will appreciate your promptness. You may wish to begin your first session with introductions and a brief get-acquainted time. Start each session by reading aloud the snapshot summary of the chapter for the day.
3. Select discussion questions and activities in advance. Note that the first question is a general question designed to get discussion going. The last question is designed to summarize the discussion. Feel free to change the order of the listed questions and to create your own questions. Allow a set amount of time for the questions and activities.
4. Remind your participants that all questions are valid as part of the learning process. Encourage their participation in discussion by saying that there are no "wrong" answers and that all input will be appreciated. Invite participants to share their thoughts, personal stories, and ideas as their comfort level allows.

5. Some questions may be more difficult to answer than others. If you ask a question and no one responds, begin the discussion by venturing an answer yourself. Then ask for comments and other answers. Remember that some questions may have multiple answers.
6. Ask the question "Why?" or "Why do you believe that?" to help continue a discussion and give it greater depth.
7. Give everyone a chance to talk. Keep the conversation moving. Occasionally you may want to direct a question to a specific person who has been quiet. "Do you have anything to add?" is a good follow-up question to ask another person. If the topic of conversation gets off track, move ahead by asking the next question in your study guide.
8. Before moving from questions to activities, ask group members if they have any questions that have not been answered. Remember that as a leader, you do not have to know all the answers. Some answers may come from group members. Other answers may even need a bit of research. Your job is to keep the discussion moving and to encourage participation.
9. Review the activity in advance. Feel free to modify it or to create your own activity. Encourage participants to try the "At home" activity.
10. Following the conclusion of the activity, close with a brief prayer, praying either the printed prayer from the study guide or a prayer of your own. If your group desires, pause for individual prayer petitions.
11. Be grateful and supportive. Thank group members for their ideas and participation.
12. You are not expected to be a "perfect" leader. Just do the best you can by focusing on the participants and the lesson. God will help you lead this group.
13. Enjoy your time together!

Suggestions for Participants

1. What you will receive from this study will be in direct proportion to your involvement. Be an active participant!
2. Please make it a point to attend all sessions and to arrive on time so that you can receive the greatest benefit.

3. Read the chapter and review the study guide questions prior to the meeting. You may want to jot down questions you have from the reading, and also answers to some of the study guide questions.
4. Be supportive and appreciative of your group leader as well as the other members of your group. You are on a journey together.
5. Your participation is encouraged. Feel free to share your thoughts about the material being discussed.
6. Pray for your group and your leader.

Introduction
Rich in the Things That Count the Most

Snapshot Summary
In the introduction to this book, the author uses the story of Jesus and Zacchaeus to highlight three riches that count the most.

Discussion Questions
1. What are some of the riches in life for which you are the most grateful?
2. What sorts of things do we tend to place value upon that perhaps really don't matter that much?
3. Is wealth "bad"? Discuss.
4. What are the results of basing happiness upon material things?
5. Is there a difference between being "content" and being "happy"? Discuss.
6. How did Zacchaeus demonstrate his faith? Discuss how a strong faith can change your life.
7. Reflect on / discuss ways that involvement in the church can enrich lives.
8. What lessons about the power of love did Zacchaeus learn from Jesus? How can the power of love change lives?

Activities
As a group: Reread the story of Zacchaeus in Luke 19:1-10. Make a list of the traits of the "old" Zacchaeus, before his encounter with

Christ, and then list the traits of the "new" Zacchaeus. What other examples have you seen, from Scripture or elsewhere, where someone experienced such a dramatic change and resolved to live a different life?

At home: Take time to count your blessings. Make a list of the riches God has provided, and give thanks each day for all you have been given.

Prayer: *Dear God, thank you for all the riches you provide. Guide us in the setting of our priorities, and help us understand that you are the Source of all good things. Grant us wisdom and generosity to use the blessings you have given us to bring blessings to others. In Jesus' name. Amen.*

Chapter 1
Rich in the Scriptures
What the Bible Teaches Us

Snapshot Summary
This chapter highlights the important lessons that can be found in the Bible.

Discussion Questions
1. Share a favorite proverb or wise saying, and explain why you find it to be special and helpful.
2. What are some of the ways Scripture makes us rich?
3. Discuss how the Bible serves as a guide for living. Tell which is your favorite Bible story, or your favorite book of the Bible, and why.
4. What are some of the things the Bible teaches us about love?
5. In what ways have you experienced God's love for you? Share how God's love has changed and guided your life.
6. What are some ways in which we can show our love to God?
7. What can prevent us from reaching out to others? What are some of the barriers we may need to overcome in order to love other people?

8. Give some reasons that you love life and treasure life as a special gift from God.

Activities
As a group: Search the Bible for treasures. Let each person or small group take a different book of the Bible and locate one or more nuggets of wisdom or guidance to enrich our lives.

At home: Devote special time each day to reading your Bible. Read from a different book of the Bible each day, or explore a particular book in depth. Underline or write out key verses and reflect on their significance for your life.

Prayer: *Dear God, thank you for all the riches contained within the Bible. Help us read the Bible often, that we may better understand and take to heart the wisdom it provides. May your Word bring us closer to you. Amen.*

Chapter 2
Rich in Soul
The Signs of a Healthy Spirit

Snapshot Summary
This chapter shows us the three signs of a healthy spirit and a healthy church: connectedness, communication, and caring.

Discussion Questions
1. Describe what it feels like to be healthy.
2. What contributes to a person's good spiritual health?
3. Discuss the benefits of maintaining a strong connectedness to church.
4. How does a healthy church help members connect with one another?
5. What requirements are necessary in order for effective communication with God?
6. Talk about different ways people communicate with God and with one another within the church setting.

7. What are some words, phrases, and/or actions that are signs of a caring Christian?
8. What does it "cost" to care for another person? Compare the costs of caring to the benefits provided.

Activities

As a group: Use newsprint or a chalkboard to draw a large church building, and inside of the building write a list of words and phrases that are healthy habits for its members. Encourage every member of the group to contribute to your list of healthy habits.

At home: Reflect on what you can do to improve the health of your church. Identify one action you can take this week toward that goal.

Prayer: *Dear God, thank you for good health, within our bodies and within the body we call the church. Help us practice and encourage habits that create good health and a rich soul. Amen.*

Chapter 3
Rich in Church
What I Love about the Church

Snapshot Summary
This chapter examines three reasons that Christians may love the church and feel indebted to it.

Discussion Questions
1. Share something about your first experiences or memories of the church. What or who has most shaped your feelings about it?
2. If you really love the church, how do you respond and act because of it?
3. What are some of the elements of a Christian lifestyle?
4. How can you help others remain in and practice a Christian lifestyle?
5. How would you respond to a friend who shared with you that while she is a Christian, and considers herself to be a spiritual person, all of her experiences with the church have been negative?

6. Share what the "power of hope" means to you.
7. When you have hope, how does it change you, and how does it make you feel?
8. How has the church enhanced your relationship with Jesus? Name some positive changes in your life.

Activities

As a group: Write a "love letter" to God, giving thanks for the blessings of the church.

At home: Think about a role or a need within your church that you can fill. Offer your help as a love offering.

Prayer: *Dear God, thank you for touching our lives and the lives of others through the church. Help us demonstrate our love for your church through our words and actions, through our commitment and our presence. Amen.*

Chapter 4
Rich in the Power of Life-Changing Words
The Sacred Power of Words

Snapshot Summary
This chapter shows why words are so powerful, and why what we say needs to be acceptable to God.

Discussion Questions
1. What makes a word powerful or influential? Give an example of words that have changed your life or that hold significant meaning for you.
2. Name a book, a poem, or a prayer that has helped you grow spiritually, and tell why the words in it are important to you.
3. Share a time when someone ministered to you with his or her words.
4. Explain what makes our words acceptable to God.
5. Talk about ways in which words can change people physically.
6. What are some emotions that can be changed or calmed through the spoken word?

7. Explain how words can change people spiritually. Give an example from your own experience.
8. Name some reasons that it is important always to choose your words wisely.

Activities
As a group: Let each person create his or her own list of phrases that are pleasing to God and can help others. When lists are completed, share examples with the rest of the group.

At home: Use your Bible to locate words from God containing promises to you. Speak to others thoughtfully and carefully this coming week, choosing your words well.

Prayer: *Dear God, thank you for words that make us better people and that can help others in times of need. Help us remember that words are sacred and contain life-changing power. Amen.*

Chapter 5
Rich in Christian Freedom
Trapped in a Prison of Our Own Making

Snapshot Summary
This chapter shows how people can become trapped in spiritual prisons of their own making, including mixed-up priorities, pride, and half-heartedness.

Discussion Questions
1. Describe what it feels like to be trapped. Share a time when you felt trapped or actually were trapped.
2. List some of the ways in which we imprison ourselves.
3. Discuss possible warning signs that indicate your priorities could be mixed up.
4. How does a person set priorities? Name some valid guidelines or questions to use in establishing priorities.
5. How does pride become dangerous and harmful?

116

6. Give some examples of the good kind of pride that is healthy and productive.
7. List the traits of half-hearted Christians. What do these Christians miss out on?
8. What lessons can we learn from Christ's encounter with the rich young ruler?

Activities
As a group: Working together or individually, create the image of a large key on a piece of paper. This key represents what sets us free. Write words or phrases on the key to illustrate the freedom we have in Jesus.

At home: Reflect on what is holding you back from a closer relationship with Jesus. Pray, asking God to give you guidance, and write down steps you'll plan to take in order to make any needed positive changes in your life.

Prayer: *Dear God, thank you for setting us free from prisons we have made for ourselves—including those of bad priorities, pride, and the half-heartedness that holds us back from serving you and others. Help us make wise choices in our lives and look to you for direction when we are lost or uncertain. Amen.*

Chapter 6
Rich in Gratitude
Jesus and Zacchaeus

Snapshot Summary
This chapter examines the blessings of gratitude and having a grateful heart.

Discussion Questions
1. Talk about a prized possession you have and what makes it special.

2. Define "genuine gratitude," and give an example of it.
3. What does it mean to celebrate the giver rather than the gift?
4. What did Jesus give to Zacchaeus that Zacchaeus needed?
5. List some of the ways Zacchaeus was changed through his encounter with Jesus.
6. How does gratitude change our relationship with God?
7. How does real gratitude affect your relationship with others?
8. Talk about what it means to have a reason for living. How does Jesus give us a new reason for living?

Activities
As a group: Create a list of creative ways to demonstrate your gratitude. Examples might include everything from washing someone's car to sending flowers to handwriting a thank-you note. Include your own personal favorites.

At home: Look for opportunities this week to show you are grateful, and act on them.

Prayer: *Dear God, thank you for changing our lives through the simple and humble act of gratitude. Help us remember our blessings and be a blessing to others. Amen.*

Chapter 7
Rich in Generosity
The Widow's Gift

Snapshot Summary
This chapter shows how trust, commitment, and love are connected to a generosity that makes us truly rich in the eyes of God.

Discussion Questions
1. Share a lesson in generosity you learned as a child. Who taught you the value of being a generous person?
2. Define what it means to be generous in the eyes of God.
3. List reasons why people often give leftovers instead of their best.

4. Explain how the widow's gift was a reflection of her trust.
5. What are some of the causes that make people lose their trust, either in God or in other people?
6. Discuss the connection between generosity and commitment.
7. How does a person become more generous? What is the connection between generosity and love?
8. What other lessons can we learn from the widow who gave so generously?

Activities
As a group: Using blank index cards, let each member of the group design and create a "dollar bill" as an affirmation and reminder of this lesson. Rather than a monetary unit, design your "dollar bill" as a form of spiritual currency. Each member may exchange dollar bills with another person in the group, along with a verbal or written affirmation using one of the key words from this lesson—*commitment, trust, love.*

At home: Make a list of some simple acts of generosity you can perform this week, and look for opportunities to put your ideas into practice.

Prayer: *Dear God, thank you for showing us what true generosity means by giving us the gift of your son, Jesus. May we be grateful to you for all you provide, and in turn be generous to our neighbors in need. Amen.*

Chapter 8
Rich in Friendship
The Rooftop Friends

Snapshot Summary
This chapter reminds us that real friends are tuned in, are persistent, and act as true servants.

Discussion Questions
1. What lessons can be learned from the story of the rooftop friends?

2. Share a time when a friend did something extraordinary to help you. How did you feel after being helped by your friend?
3. How does a person become rich in friendship? List some of the keys.
4. What often prevents us from being sensitive to the needs of others? What should we do in order to be "tuned in"?
5. Talk about an incident in your life in which you were very persistent. What motivated you, and what was the outcome?
6. Give your own explanation of what it means to be God's servant.
7. Think about your friends. What qualities do you look for and expect in a person you call a friend?
8. Reflect on / discuss what it means to have Jesus as your friend.

Activities
As a group: Create a top ten list of what it means to be a true friend.

At home: This week, be a real friend to someone who really needs your friendship, or who just may need someone with whom to talk.

Prayer: *Dear God, thank you for friends who enrich our lives. May we seek to be a friend at all times. Help us treasure our friendships, both old and new, and continue to nurture them. Amen.*

Chapter 9
Rich in Real Life
I Hope You Live All of Your Life

Snapshot Summary
This chapter looks at three ingredients of real life—a healthy love for self, a healthy love of others, and a healthy love for God.

Discussion Questions
1. What do you enjoy most about life?
2. Discuss what it means to live life to the fullest.
3. What can sometimes prevent people from accepting the abundant life that Jesus offers?

4. Discuss why some people really live, while others just exist or cope.
5. Talk about the traits of a healthy love of self.
6. Give a summary of our calling as Christians. What does God want from us? How does God want us to spend our time and talents?
7. How do you develop and nurture a healthy Christian love for others? What does it take to become a person who is comfortable expressing love?
8. Name some of the ways we can demonstrate our love for God.

Activities
As a group: Use art supplies to create a classroom banner with the words found in Luke 10:27. Some group members may use their Bibles to identify additional verses you can add to the banner.

At home: Reflect upon your own life. What do you like about it? What don't you like? What needs to be changed? What actions are you going to take?

Prayer: *Dear God, thank you for life, the gift that money cannot buy. Help us treasure this gift and use our time wisely and for your glory. Amen.*

Chapter 10
Rich in "Because Of" Faith
Do You Have an "In Order To" Faith or a "Because Of" Faith?

Snapshot Summary
This chapter encourages Christians to rejoice always, to pray without ceasing, and to give thanks in all circumstances.

Discussion Questions
1. Share a spiritual "lightbulb moment" from your life.
2. Explain what "responsive gratitude" means to you, and give an example of it.
3. Explain the difference between an "In Order To" faith and a "Because Of" faith.

4. How are Bartimaeus and the apostle Paul examples of responsive gratitude?
5. What is it about Christianity that motivates Christians to rejoice?
6. Talk about what it means to pray without ceasing.
7. As you are comfortable doing so, share something about the way or ways in which you prefer to pray. What best enables you to talk with God?
8. What enables Christians to be able to give thanks in all circumstances?

Activities
As a group: Make a list comparing characteristics of an "In Order To" faith with characteristics of a "Because Of" faith. Comparisons might include actions, words, and attitudes, for example.

At home: Reflect on your own faith. What genuine effect does your faith have upon who you are, what you do, and how you relate to God and others?

Prayer: *Dear God, thank you for everything you do for us. You are awesome, and we praise you for your love and kindness. Help us rejoice always, pray without ceasing, and give thanks to you for blessing us so richly. Amen.*

Chapter 11
Rich in Mind, Body, and Spirit
Jesus Increased in Wisdom and in Stature and in Favor with God and People

Snapshot Summary
This chapter offers encouragement to help children grow in mind, in body, and in spirit.

Discussion Questions
1. List and discuss the different types of "precious cargo" God entrusts to us.
2. Give some reasons why the precious cargo in our lives is sometimes lost or damaged.

3. Do you agree with the author's assertion that the Christian home needs to be a top priority? Explain your reasoning.
4. What obstacles and issues do children face today? In what ways do we all bear some responsibility regarding children, even if we aren't parents ourselves?
5. List some simple ways we can help children grow in wisdom.
6. Explain what it means to grow in stature. How does this occur?
7. How can using the "measuring stick of Christ" help guide our lives and our decisions?
8. How can we help bring our children into a closer relationship with Jesus Christ?

Activities
As a group: Ask class members to draw either a boat or car that represents their life. Have them fill it, by words or pictures, with all the precious cargo that God has entrusted to them.

At home: Focus this week on talking to, listening to, or helping your child or a child in your family. If you are not a parent, you might decide to spend some time talking with someone who is, in order to learn more about children's and parents' needs. Be aware of the needs of children and how you can help them grow in body, in mind, and in spirit.

Prayer: *Dear God, thank you for entrusting us with so many different varieties of precious cargo. Help us treasure our children and encourage them to grow in faith. Amen.*

Chapter 12
Rich in the Risen Christ
When the Risen Christ Comes Looking for Us

Snapshot Summary
This chapter looks at three powerful ways the risen Christ meets us and helps us today.

Discussion Questions
1. Talk about a person who influenced your faith and helped you grow spiritually.
2. Share a time when your words got you into trouble.
3. In what ways are Christians often like Simon Peter? Describe some of the similarities.
4. What are some of the lessons we learn from Christ's encounter with Simon Peter in John 21?
5. Share a time when the risen Christ came to bring you love when you needed it.
6. Describe the love that Jesus had for Simon Peter and also for us today.
7. How does it feel to need forgiveness? How does it feel after you have been forgiven?
8. Discuss some of the many ways Jesus provides direction for our lives.

Activities
As a group: Search the Bible for examples of how the risen Christ helps us today based upon how Jesus helped his followers after his resurrection.

At home: Keep your eyes open this week for examples of how the risen Christ ministers to you and to others.

Prayer: *Dear God, thank you for providing us with your love, forgiveness, and direction in our lives—at all times, including when we need it the most. Help us be your servants and be a blessing to others during this coming week. Amen.*

Chapter 13
Rich in Easter Faith
Jesus and Mary Magdalene

Snapshot Summary
This chapter shows how Easter gives us a sense of peace, a sense of humor, and a sense of mission.

Discussion Questions

1. What do you believe were Mary's thoughts and feelings as she walked to the tomb on Easter morning?
2. When you visit the grave of a loved one, how do you feel? What do you think about?
3. Complete the following sentence: "The good news of Easter is . . . "
4. Discuss the reasons why Easter gives Christians a sense of peace.
5. What do you personally need to do in order to feel God's presence and to feel at peace?
6. Discuss the benefits of having a good sense of humor.
7. What do you consider to be your mission in life?
8. Discuss the sense of mission that Easter gives us as Christians.

Activities

As a group: Using art supplies and a card about the size of a standard business card, create your own Easter card highlighting the gifts of Easter. Carry your card with you as a daily reminder of Easter.

At home: Reflect on Easter and how it comes not just once a year, but every day, for believers. Celebrate the joy of Easter this week!

Prayer: *Dear God, thank you for the richness that comes with an Easter faith. Help us always remember the truth of Easter and celebrate it every day of the year. Amen.*

Chapter 14
Rich in Commitment to Christ
Jesus and Bartimaeus

Snapshot Summary

This chapter explores the lessons in grit, grace, and gratitude found in the encounter of Jesus and Bartimaeus.

Discussion Questions

1. Share a time when you felt the presence of God and experienced a special moment of faith.

2. Discuss the similarities in the story of the man who insisted on being baptized and the story of Bartimaeus.
3. What do you most admire about Bartimaeus?
4. Share a time when you showed true grit and "seized the moment."
5. What can we learn about God's grace from the story of Bartimaeus?
6. When you feel a sense of gratitude, what does it motivate you to do?
7. In what ways is the story of Bartimaeus a lesson in gratitude?
8. How did your reading and/or discussion of this book personally enrich you? What additional insights or questions would you like to explore?

Activities

As a group: Have a "graduation" time for members of your small group. Create personalized "Rich in the Things That Count the Most" completion certificates; then exchange them and write messages of gratitude and encouragement.

At home: Reflect on your reading of this book and on this small-group experience. What lessons did you learn about the true riches and blessings of life? What changes do you see taking place in your life?

Prayer: *Dear God, thank you for blessing us so richly, in so many ways. Thank you for the gift of your son, Jesus Christ, and for loving us always, come what may. Help us see and be grateful for the true riches of life that you place all around us, and empower us to be your faithful followers, that we may bless others as you have blessed us. Amen.*